D1666448

QUANTITY SALES

The Road Taken and other books from The Local History Company are available at special quantity discounts for bulk purchases or sales promotions, premiums, fund raising, or educational use by corporations, institutions, and other organizations. Special imprints, messages, and excerpts can also be produced to meet your specific needs.

For details, please contact us at:

Special Sales

The Local History Company
112 North Woodland Road
Pittsburgh, PA 15232
412-362-2294
info@TheLocalHistoryCompany.com
www.TheLocalHistoryCompany.com
Please specify how you intend to use the books (e.g. promotion, resale, fund raising, etc.)

INDIVIDUAL SALES

To order this book, use a copy of the order form at the back of this book, or for an up-to-date listing of our books and information on how to order, contact us at:

Sales

The Local History Company
112 NORTH Woodland Road
Pittsburgh, PA 15232
412-362-2294
info@TheLocalHistoryCompany.com
www.TheLocalHistoryCompany.com

The Road Taken

A Journey in Time Down Pennsylvania Route 45

By

Joan Morse Gordon

with a foreword by
Edward K. Muller

The Local History Company
publishers of history and heritage

Pittsburgh, Pennsylvania, USA

The Road Taken
A Journey In Time Down Pennsylvania Route 45
With a Foreword by Edward K. Muller
Copyright © 2002 by Joan Morse Gordon

Published by
The Local History Company
112 North Woodland Road
Pittsburgh, PA 15232
www.TheLocalHistoryCompany.com
info@TheLocalHistoryCompany.com

The name "The Local History Company", "Publishers of History and Heritage", and its logo are trademarks of The Local History Company.

Design by Navta Associates, Inc.

Library of Congress Cataloging-in-Publication Data

Gordon, Joan Morse
    The road taken : a journey in time down Pennsylvania Route 45 / by
  Joan Morse Gordon ; with a foreword by Edward K. Muller.
        p.   cm.
    Includes bibliographical references and index.
    ISBN 0-9711835-1-1 (acid-free paper)
    1. Pennsylvania--Description and travel. 2. Pennsylvania--History,
  Local. 3. Pennsylvania Route 45 Region (Pa.)--History. 4. Historic sites-
  -Pennsylvania--Pennsylvania Route 45 Region. 5. Huntingdon County
  (Pa.)--History, Local. 6. Centre County (Pa.)--History, Local. 7. Union
  County (Pa.)--History, Local. 8. Montour County (Pa.)--History, Local.
  I. Title.

F149 .G67 2001
974.8--dc21

                                   2001003797

Printed in Canada

 # Dedication

To Jeanne Krochalis and Robert Frank
who opened their hearts and home
and showed me the way

J.M.G.

Acknowledgments

My profound gratitude to all the people who helped along the way . . . those I've profiled and those behind the scene. Invaluable was the interest and cooperation of these individuals not acknowledged elsewhere in the text: Barbara Brueggebors, then of the *Centre Daily Times*, Gladys Murray, then at the Centre County Library, and Jacqueline Melander at the Centre County Historical Society; at State College Elizabeth Smith, Ron Filippelli, Sandra Stelts, Peirce Lewis, Roy Buck, William B. and Bette White; in Lewisburg, Katie Faull and Nancy Weyant.

On the home front at the University of Pittsburgh where I received my Masters of Fine Arts in Creative Nonfiction, I am indebted particularly to David Walton, Ann Sutherland Harris, Myron Taube, and to my committee members, Patsy Sims, Edward Muller, Richard Tobias and Lee Gutkind.

And in the greater world a thank you to my children, Ann Morse, Fuzzbee Morse, Rich Gordon and Tom Gordon, who spurred me on from afar with their encouragement and love.

Table of Contents

⌂ Foreword

For the past few generations Americans have enjoyed the convenience of traveling at high speeds along limited access Interstate highways. Riding comfortably in vehicles outfitted with numerous amenities, travelers see passing landscapes that vary with the region of the country, hilly uplands, mountains, flat and rolling farmlands, unending deserts. However, despite these obvious variations, there is often a sense of disconnectedness from the landscape and a sameness to this kind of travel. The Interstate highways adhere to federal standards. They are never too steep, winding, or narrow. Put the car and mind in cruise control and speed along. Similarly, the rest areas, service plazas, and business complexes at exits all look the same. Landscaping looks like it has all come from the same pattern book, all pine bark mulch and juniper bushes. Food and drinks match the blandness and convenience of the highway. And, corporate chains with their recognizable, readily interpreted signs dominate these oases of gas stations, restaurants, and motels. Travel along the Interstate network is meant merely to get to one's destination.

There is another America awaiting the traveler, if he or she takes the time to experience it. The traveler must abandon the Interstates and journey along the older U.S. and state routes that traverse what was once called "the countryside." In the words of William Least Heat Moon, these are the "blue highways" on one's map. Here, the traveling is slower; the roads may be steep, winding, and narrow. One must slow down for towns and villages, watch for intersecting roads with vehicles entering and exiting, and accommodate slowly moving trucks, farm equipment, or even horse drawn buggies in some locales. The heightened alertness of the driver and the intimacy of the highway with the countryside allow one to see the landscape in great detail. The richness of house and barn architecture, fencing, vegetation, animals (wild and domestic), signs (new and abandoned), and even people register in the mind. A greater variety of shops and services invite the traveler to stop and linger, but they involve risk, too. One cannot be certain of the quality of food, accommodation, or service. Culinary specialties may pleasantly surprise, but they may disappoint as well. And, most of all, one meets "real" people, encountering them in their own environments, not in the sanitized, homogenized world of corporate spaces.

It is the people of Route 45 in central Pennsylvania who interest Joan Morse Gordon. Route 45 is a "blue highway." It follows one of Pennsylvania's long southwest to northeast narrow valleys, in this case actually two valleys, running between steep ridges on either side. Its countryside of another, older America–the barns, houses, and small towns–initially attracted Gordon. The self-contained geography of the valleys seemed to make this place manageable. And, with time she learned that it was populated by a number of endearing characters. People and landscape are, of course, always intimately entwined. People shape the landscape, and are shaped by it. But Gordon's exploration of the Penns and Buffalo valleys centers on the folks who live or once lived there. She introduces the reader to Aaron Levy, the Jewish immigrant who founded Aaronsburg in the late eighteenth century; Bruce Teeple, curator of the local historical museum; woodworker and dowser Randall Stover; Linda Buchanan who bought, preserved, and lived at a log cabin complex on the site of a Revolutionary era fort and frontier settlement; Eric and Claudia Sarnow who came to the valley to open a gourmet French restaurant; Marie Musser who published her first book at age 88; the Nebraska Amish family of Sam and Barbara Zook; and many others. Moving from person to person, Gordon weaves together the valleys' history and present lifestyles. Many of her folk are descendants of families who settled there generations ago. They either never left or only temporarily left before returning to the safety and comfort of this familiar homeland. Others sought out the isolation, slow pace, and intimate community of these valleys, hemmed in by protective mountains, far from the state's metropolitan influences, and untouched by the Interstate highways that inevitably let in the outside world.

Remote as the Penns and Buffalo valleys may seem, they are not immune to the modern world's impulses. In truth, they never have been free of change. In Gordon's narrative, a mining company wants to strip mine limestone, and it is pitted against archaeologists, trout fishermen, cavers, environmentalists, and residents who wish to preserve the limestone caves, trout streams, and valleys' quality of life. South of the mining site, suburbs of the rapidly growing urban complex of State

College and The Pennsylvania State University are spilling into Penns Valley. In her book Gordon offers a glimpse of this blue highway countryside even as time, suburban development, and economic imperatives inexorably alter it. She provides a personal and sympathetic portrait. She also makes a compelling case for slowing down, making a detour from one's normal itinerary, and exploring other blue highways and their surrounding countrysides across America.

We bemoan the sprawl of suburban development eating up rural land dozens of miles from the center of our metropolitan areas. We lament sprawl's sameness from region to region, its lack of form and a center, and its unfriendly environment for pedestrians. We ritually decry the loss of farm land, the supposed bedrock of America. At the same time, we no longer really know the countryside and its people. We no longer know much about what we are losing to sprawl. The rural landscape and its people impede what we call progress. Curiously, they are becoming more and more remote from us despite our invasion of their spaces. Gordon asks us to rediscover this other America. Perhaps this discovery will heighten our sensitivity and concern about the destruction of the countryside. Perhaps, we may be moved to rethink the path we are taking.

Edward K. Muller
Professor of History
Director of Urban Studies
University of Pittsburgh

Route 45

INTRODUCTION: A ROAD
OF MY OWN

For 14 years, early in the summer, I would load up the car in Pittsburgh and make my annual pilgrimage east to a little house in the Berkshires near the New York-Massachusetts border. The trip of almost 500 miles took me two days. Part of the leisurely rhythm of my journey was finding a pleasant place to spend the night. Ideally the small hotel or inn or bed and breakfast should be more than half way to my destination, making my transition at the far end gentler and less tiring. Heading back west, it became a ritual to turn off Interstate 80 at exit 33, a spot in the middle of the Pennsylvania map where most roads and streams and hills appear to cascade southwesterly all the way down to Maryland. I headed south briefly, and then west on 642 until it branches off at the start of Route 45, which curves southwestward until it ends 100 miles and five counties later at Route 22.

Over the years I came to think of this road as my own. The route lies in a ridge-valley configuration formed over 250 million years ago. At one point in geologic history it was a part of the Acadian Mountains in Ireland, before tectonic plate movement shoved it to our side of the Atlantic. The road ambles along this downward sweeping arc following a sheltered fertile limestone valley. I was told by a wise geographer that Route 45 goes from nowhere to nowhere, that it begins and ends with a whimper, because there are no landmarks, no towns of note, nothing historical to anchor it at either end. Somehow that idea was perversely appealing. This road of mine, I was pleased to note, was no thruway.

This was a byway, a road less traveled, less transient, with a greater sense of permanence, of roots. I like roots, mine being fairly shallow.

> *"Roads no longer lead to places; they are places. The road offered a journey into the unknown that could end up allowing us to discover who we were and where we belonged,"*

says John Brinckerhoff Jackson in *A Sense of PLACE . . . A Sense of TIME*, speaking of roads in general. And he cautions that roads, which come from the outside world, could conceivably bring in strangers and strange ideas.

One year, after just a few miles of driving on 45, I was aware of a feeling I had experienced there before, a comforting sense of time-lessness and enduring stability. At this edgy moment in history as we approached the millennium, timelessness itself was seductive—like an unlined face, a Shangri-La, a Brigadoon. Altogether, a safe place to be. Driving along through rolling farmland, I noted that silos and steeples were still the tallest man-made edifices. Majestic forebay barns with sheltering overhangs, many mysteriously flaunting Gothic windows, dwarfed the modest farmhouses and called me to investigate further. The towns through which I passed were well tended. Mature maple and black walnut trees met and shaded town centers. Direction signs at crossroads indicated springs, forges, mills and caves nearby, all echoes of the past. More important was what wasn't there: billboards, graffiti, used car lots, and even worse, auto graveyards and adult movie shacks, typical despoilers of the landscape of so many highways today. If any existed, these eyesores didn't confront me and I apparently chose to overlook them.

I would ask myself, while driving through the tiny towns and open farmland, who were the people who first came here? What brought them to this valley in the middle of nowhere in the first place? What were they hoping to find? And did they find it? Who stayed on, who left, and why? And what connection, if any, had I as an outsider to this place? Would I ever choose to stay and take root?

I limited my time in the East for a number of summers to try to answer these questions. I traversed the route's five counties, settling in for weeks at a time by cat-sitting, and friend-making, researching local history and geology, visiting county historical societies, attending house tours and fairs and auctions and dinners and meetings, observing and questioning and listening. I didn't pretend this road was my home. It was a way-station, a place to rest and refresh, to marvel at the self-sufficiency of those who inhabit it, and to provide a valuable perspective to this born and bred city person.

I soon found so much rich material that I narrowed my focus to a smaller area of Route 45 in Penns and Buffalo Valleys, and spent extended time with a few individuals who lived there and whose lives were peripherally related. In them, descendants of early settlers, long time residents and recent arrivals, all devoted to the valley, I discerned even in their diversity, an essential need for the proper environment in which to survive. One characteristic they all shared was a willingness to work hard. The early settlers were seeking freedom from religious and political persecution; the more recent arrivals were escaping from contemporary urban pressures. Had they found what they wanted? I would see.

I learned that population in the villages and hamlets along the road has remained the same for more than 100 years. Stagnant numbers actually mean that people have been leaving. Ordinarily, population increases at the rate of ten percent every decade. The only exception, save for the escaped city dwellers, is the influx of the Amish, whose principal livelihood is farming. They find the isolation of these valleys compatible with their life style, since they prefer not to rub elbows too heavily with the outside world, and have managed to retain their unique identity all through this country and beyond for over 200 years. With their propensity for large families, the Amish have overpopulated themselves out of their former territories further east and south. Since they traditionally bestow farmland as a heritage on their children, they've outgrown Lancaster County to the east and are now clambering over the mountains out of Kishacoquillas Valley to the south, where they "came up, settled, multiplied and subdued the earth," says Dr. Peirce Lewis, a distinguished geographer at Penn State. Today, many Amish have bought up farms in Penns Valley around Coburn, Aaronsburg and Millheim.

Dr. Lewis expects the area to be "heavy duty" Amish country soon. The surnames one comes across most frequently are Beachy, Peachy, Zook, Beiler, Hostetler, Stolzfus and Yoder. Lewis describes the newly arrived Amish as "hermit crabs," converting an old farm or a California ranch house to their own needs. Updating a biblical passage, "Be not tethered with an equal yoke," the Amish translate it to mean, "don't you plug into any electrical or gas supply." Frequently, they will build a new secondary house, a *Grossdaadi Haus*, for the old folks who, on their retirement, relinquish the main house to a married son or daughter.

Throughout Penns Valley, Amish families in their distinctive clothing can be seen on main and back roads driving their horse-drawn buggies with varied tops in white, yellow, grey, brown and black, each color denoting an internal diversity in their beliefs. In the fields the more worldly Amish yoke up a team of horses to pull their tractors. In fact, the horse sets the limits of the Amish horizon for both labor and travel. Their old-fashioned methods of dealing with the land have enhanced the illusion to outsiders that so-called "progress" has not touched the valleys, although farming itself has altered the land irrevocably.

Early European settlers in Pennsylvania were Quakers and other persecuted English who came with William Penn from 1682 to 1710. Next were the Welsh and a few Scots from 1710 to 1730. Pietist Protestant Germans from the Palatinate arrived between 1735 and 1750 and settled southeastern Pennsylvania in a solid band from Allentown to Gettysburg. Who were these Palatines who survived onslaught after onslaught? There were some Flemish and French Huguenots among them who had escaped Louis XIV's persecution of French Protestants. Mainly the Palatines were Rhenish farmers, vineyard workers and craftsmen, who were heavily tithed and taxed while working the land for large landholders and the nobility. Eventually this group, after new lands opened up to settlers, spread west into Penns Valley.

According to Eli Faber in *A Time for Planting*, early America was not entirely free of prejudice. "The English regarded the Germans in the hinterland of Pennsylvania as obtuse and dull, comical and ridiculous . . . Appraising the German settlers in 1764, Benjamin Franklin wondered, 'Should the Palatine Boors be suffered to swarm into our settlements, and by herding together establish their language and manners, to the exclusion of ours?' "

It is the Palatine Germans and Swiss who have had the biggest impact on Route 45 and whose descendants have prevailed. I have come to learn that the lack of information or interest in their roots is not uncommon to long settled families in these parts. Although unconsciously ingrained in their former ethnic work ethic, religion, and moral values, they have long ago severed any conscious or direct link with the Old World. The style of their homes, methods of farming and general mode of life are mirrors of the past modified by the influence of settlers from other parts of Europe. Unlike second or third generation offspring of immigrants who cluster in heavily ethnic neighborhoods in cities, with churches onion-domed or medieval, who celebrate in a stopped time ritual with food and dance and song the traditions of their forebears, the citizens along Route 45 tend to think of themselves as village or township or county residents; Pennsylvanians or Americans first.

If you stop at the old Stover cemetery between Woodward and Aaronsburg on Route 45 and walk amongst the graves you can see the evolution of Germanic names from Stuver to Stober or Stover, and Bauer to Bower; a gradual transformation into the melting pot that forged a new nation. Tombstone materials change with time from simple red schist to solid white marble. These names plus Hosterman, Musser, Boob or Boop, Yoder, Weaver, Weber and Wolfe recur throughout the valley's history. Their descendants live on here today.

The location of the valleys, bypassed by Interstate 80 today, cut off by restricting ridges then and now, has left the valley people isolated from the mainstream. And here, in America, consciously or not, their patterns of living relate back to the old country where their roots were in the land and their education limited. The ideas of Emerson, Thoreau and Jefferson don't seem to have penetrated the ridges to these valleys, any more than the thoughts of Goethe and Kant reached them in the Palatine. Politically conservative, and yet voting as Democrats, steady attendees at their Lutheran and Reform churches, they are not fundamentalists, nor adherents of the religious right as we understand these terms today. Many of the valley residents are without passion, except for family and possibly the National Rifle Association, as evidenced by an occasional bumper sticker sporting:

God, Guns and Guts
Made America
Let's Keep
All Three

Some have never been out of the valley, even those on the staff of Penn State or Bucknell, who regularly encounter other cultures, and may never have tasted foreign food other than fast food pizza or tacos. Many are not readers. Their principal exposure to culture is through television, their music is generic church and country. They grow farther away from their past, many not even knowing from which ethnic roots they branched. Secure in their isolation, the status quo prevails.

Living among the valley mainstream are some free spirits, individuals following their own stars. They range in age from the twenties to the nineties. I have been especially drawn to them. I have spent time with a few Amish families, a few Mennonites, university people, townspeople, cavers, miners, librarians, historians, new blood, old blood, yuppies, and a mountain man. There's a 92 year old lady whose first book was published when she was 88 and who recently added a room to her house to accommodate her new Nordic Track. And a woman who lives and farms on the site of Lower Fort, which was attacked by Indians in the 1780s, who thrives amidst her books and music in a one room house with no indoor plumbing. And a man whose job is maintenance but whose passion is history.

The town of Aaronsburg, located plumb in the middle of the state, and narrowly strung out along Route 45, has a fascinating past and recent history. Aaron Levy, a Jewish immigrant from Holland whose gesture of friendship to the town's Christian church fathers brought this obscure village international attention 150 years later, founded it in 1786. Today, a perceived threat to the quality of life in and around Aaronsburg has once again drawn a wide circle of attention. Mobilization for protest is centered on a recently started limestone mining operation in Penns Valley. How have the citizens reacted? I have spent time looking at all sides of the conflict.

I have also made some detours along the road, tangentially tied in the past to Aaron Levy. One involved Joseph Priestley, discoverer of oxygen, founder of Unitarianism, and friend of Thomas Jefferson, who escaped a Royalist mob in England and settled in an area a little south of my road. His sons almost convinced the English poets Coleridge and Southey to settle here in an aborted attempt to establish a Utopian community.

Another by-road led to a group of French Loyalists who set up a village, a Paris-on-the-Susquehanna, during the height of the French Revolution. It was intended as a haven for Marie Antoinette, who, unfortunately had lost her head before their log Queen's House was fully constructed. These were urban sophisticates escaping from immediate peril seeking to duplicate their home environment and carve a Versailles out of the wilderness, a far cry from the reality they encountered.

William Least Heat Moon, in *PrairyErth*, says, "To see and know a place is a contemplative act. It means emptying our mind and letting what is there, in all its multiplicity and endless variety, come in." The road, Route 45, is both a metaphor and a place to me. I am a city person whose life has been shaped and filled by the external stimuli of predigested "culture," removed from the necessities of survival or hands-on labor, somewhat like the early transient French and English who didn't take root. The more I've opened my mind to this place, the greater has been my insight into the rhythm of life in the valleys. I've been looking at old blood to see if they're stuck in the past, or manage to keep the juices flowing; and new blood to see how they've settled in, and where and how they infuse new ideas. My hope is to examine their values, understand their way of life, weigh their need for roots, and having found them, re-examine my own.

Chapter 1

THE MUSEUM VISIT

On a clear, bright, sunny autumn afternoon in Aaronsburg, Pennsylvania in 1993, puffy white clouds scud across a Tiepolo blue sky. I take long strides to keep pace with Bruce Teeple. Tall, handsome, forty-ish, fully mustachioed, thick dark straight-haired and sharp-nosed, he looks for all the world as if he should be standing stiffly on guard at Buckingham Palace in a scarlet British Grenadier's uniform and beaver hat. Instead he casually wears full suspendered denim coveralls and a Teamsters Union Local # 8 baseball cap.

Barbara Brueggebors, of the *Centre Daily Times* in State College, a former editor who specialized in Centre County news, advised me to see Bruce if I wanted a good grounding on Aaronsburg and the surrounding area in Penns Valley.

Aaronsburg (pop. 680) lies on the midpoint of Route 45, which is 100 miles long and traverses the five counties of which Centre is the center. There's no change in the number of residents, summer or winter, except for a few weekend bed and breakfasters. Here is where I planned to start my exploration of the full length of the road, its history, its people, past and present.

Bruce, his wife, Michelle, and two teen-age daughters, Alice and Jane, live on East Plum Street where we meet, a short walk from the Penns Valley Historical Association, which I will refer to as the Museum. He serves as volunteer curator when he is not at work in the Maintenance

Department at Penn State. "I haul concrete," he tells me as he unlocks the door. I duck my head as we descend into the low-ceilinged basement of the former Evangelical United Brethren Church where the Museum is housed. Outside I'd noticed that its tower was covered with fish scale shingles and was sorely in need of a coat of paint. Upstairs, with its high ceiling and sun shining through bright stained glass windows of the former sanctuary, is the Aaronsburg Library. Downstairs, temporary partitions separate the crowded historical exhibits. The walls are almost invisible, covered as they are from floor to ceiling with all kinds of memorabilia. Lighting between the exposed ceiling pipes is makeshift. Nevertheless Teeple's enthusiasm is undimmed.

"Who started the museum?" I inquire.

"My predecessor, a school teacher named Ralph Beahm," he replies. "He was the type of guy who used to bug everybody. 'Why don't you give this or that to the museum?' He ticked off a lot of people, needling them all the time. Then he passed away. It was like a yard sale down here. All the Indian artifacts were in a toolbox. These documents were under a sink in the back room, about two hundred of them. So our big priority has been encapsulating all the paper items."

As we start the tour I point to a stone tool labeled 8,500 BC.

"Yep. This has been a happy hunting ground for about 10,000 years. You're standing on some of the oldest geology or geological forms on earth right now. One of the things we do with history is try to understand why things are the way they are. I have a little road show when I go to schools or scout groups or whatever . . . I hold up one of the things and say 'What's this?' Kids'll say, 'A rock.' 'What kind of rock?' 'I don't know.' 'It's Ordovician limestone,' I tell them, 'the heart and soul of Centre County. This is why the farmers came here. It's an indication of good farming soil.'"

The early settlers burned chunks of the blue-grey stone to make quicklime to sweeten their fields and to use in mixing mortar for building with bricks. And the early industrialists came because they needed limestone as a flux in ironmaking.

"Now there's another side to this," he says, meaning the stone. He flips it over. "Wow! Fossils? Right? And seashells on the seashore. What are they doing up here? At one time, I tell the students, this whole region was under the ocean.

"Another thing we question is why things are the way they are. For

Bruce Teeple, Penns Valley Historical Association Curator. Photo by Joan Morse Gordon.

example, why are the mountains going from the southwest to the northeast in this state? That's from the successive bumpings at one point by the African continent up against what is now Delaware. The successive bumpings are what created the mountains. Where the mountains are now was where the valleys used to be and vice versa. Everything's been reversed. These are extremely old mountains and were a lot higher than the Rockies or the Alps or Himalayas are today, but they've been worn down through various forces in nature."

Bruce's description reminds me that all through the middle section of Pennsylvania, diagonal ridge-valley formations produce a gentle accordioned landscape whose low hills act as isolating barriers between one valley and the next. *A Concise Historical Atlas of Pennsylvania* describes the Ridge and Valley region as "a distinctive belt of long, wooded ridges and broad agricultural valleys that sweeps diagonally through the heart of Pennsylvania." The landscape, being slow to change, has "taken on a kind of antique look, unusual in the fast-moving America of the late twentieth century." The authors conclude that with family farms surviving and towns unchanged "this quiet, bucolic, small-town environment . . . is increasingly attractive to urban refugees," of which I'm apparently one.

Our tour moves along.

"There were three major Indian groups in Pennsylvania during the time of the European invasion," Bruce continues, pointing at a large map of Pennsylvania on the wall. "The Leni Lenapes and Delawares were here (pointing east), the Susquehannas were essentially here (midstate) and the Monongahelas there (west). All of them, for the most part, died out. The Shawnees were brought into this area at the request of the Seven Nations and are basically the last group of Indians in Pennsylvania up until about 1800."

"The Delawares, for the most part, ended up out in Kansas, and the Susquehannas and the Conestogas and various subgroupings were massacred over the years, or died from disease, primarily measles and tuberculosis, which they caught from the Europeans during the 1700s.

"Now, these artifacts," pointing to some delicate bones arranged in a semi-circle in a glass case, "It's the whole notion of jewelry or ornamentation. People today go to the store and they see something shiny and pretty and they buy it. To the people who made these things they had some personal meaning. These were bird bones. Birds have hollow bones—that's why they fly. You can string them together and make a necklace such as this. Use seashells, for example, or somebody's tooth. It had some special meaning to you. And you can imagine the craftsmanship going into something like fashioning this with a bone or stone or a wooden awl or drill. We don't know a lot about these people because we kicked them out before we had a chance to understand them. That's kind of sad."

Arriving at a small glass case, he continues. "There are certain ways of decorating pottery—bark incised, pressing the pot against the tree bark; textile incised, pressing against deerskin cloth; and the stick, or reed or thumbnail or flint incised. Now, we have an example here. This is a pipe bowl. You can see the decoration somebody made with his or her thumbnail. This flips kids out. And this I really enjoy. This other one is corncob incised." I marvel at the miniature size. "You're not talking Silver Queen corn like we have today. What we've done in hybridizing our corn is in a sense retard our gene pool. We have to go back to the original Teosinte corn out in the plains of central Mexico looking for the original plants and try to reverse the genetic strength of the corn. But look at the size of those kernels. See how small they were? A whole husk! Only half an inch long!"

We move from the mores of the native to the tactics of the settler in clearing his land. Teeple hands me a stone implement, which I mistake for a tomahawk. "This is a hand ax as opposed to a tomahawk, a war ax. This is not ceremonial—it's worn down. Now how in god's name are you cutting down trees, this virgin timber, with something like this? Those trees are as big around in diameter as this room. What you did was you girdled the tree. You took a strip of bark, and just chopped it off all the way around the tree. You did three or four of those trees in the fall. The leaves don't come out in the spring because the trees have effectively been killed off. So with three or four trees cleared, you have almost a whole acre where sunlight can filter through and your plants can grow. That's a nice alternative to slash and burn which a lot of people did, too."

As we slowly move through the crowded space, bumping into dummies in costume and an old His Master's Voice phonograph, Bruce tells me that at the time the Europeans were coming into Pennsylvania in the 1770s there were three forts in Penns Valley: Upper Fort, also known as Old Fort, was near Centre Hall on General Potter's land; Middle Fort or Watson's Fort was out near the current Penns Valley High School; and Lower Fort was down near Woodward cave. Since this central part of Pennsylvania was the frontier, armed protection was required. Bruce suggests I meet a family named Buchanan who lives on the site of Lower Fort.

According to the terms of one of the many treaties Europeans made with the Native Americans in 1763, white settlement was to be limited to no more than one mile north of Penns Creek. "But," Bruce explains, "human nature being what it is, we went a little further and a little further. Understandably these people get ticked off and we had Amerind raiding parties coming down from New York State."

One of the worst massacres was near the Wilkes Barre area. The Forty Fort massacre sent shock waves all over the area. There were raiding parties and massacres throughout central Pennsylvania. One occurred in the town of Penns Creek and two in Penns Valley. The Jacob Stanford family was attacked and scalped in their isolated cabin on the other side of Centre Hall, and some local Provincial soldiers were wiped out on a road called Indian Lane right off Route 45. Their modest grave can still be seen there today.

"Afterward, they had a thing called the Great Runaway, something out of Monty Python. The settlers tore off up over the mountains after the massacres. They were essentially Scotch-Irish squatters who had no legal title to the land. They didn't come back for nine years. Well, here come these Germans up from Lancaster and Lebanon, for the most part second generation. They have legal title that was granted by dispersion by the state. In the early years of Centre County the court dockets were filled up with lawsuits between squatters and Germans. But these Germans are holding documents saying, 'Hey, I'fe got legal title to zis land. You can't take dat away from me. Ve keep dat in da family. Dey'll never take our land avay from us.' " As I discovered later, the Germans invariably won.

In the intervening years, as a result of the American Revolution, land had been expropriated in the name of the people. As a result of the war the government had no money in its treasury. Revolutions were expensive and veterans were owed back pay. The recently discharged veterans were offered, in lieu of back pay, roughly 300-acre undeveloped tracts, called officers' warrants.

Bruce continues. "Now if you're a veteran living in the eastern part of the state where most of the people were, east or south, during the Revolution, are you going to want to farm 300 acres sight unseen? Uhn uhn! Or are you going to take the money and run? Most of them took the money and ran. They sold their warrants to the Germans and land speculators such as Aaron Levy who founded Aaronsburg. He's an interesting character who was a salt hoarder during the revolution. His base of operations was just north of Sunbury in a town called Northumberland."

"Tell me about salt hoarding," I ask Bruce.

"You needed salt to preserve food. Salt licks were harvested up in New York State and the salt was brought down the Susquehanna River to be sold. Well, Levy would buy it all up at a wholesale price and then he'd hoard it and wait for the price to go up. That's how he made his money. After the Revolution he had all this money and he could buy the land off of these veterans." I would pursue his facts later.

"Now there were also a lot of people who were first and second generation. James Duncan's father was a David Duncan. They lived down in Lancaster or Lebanon, in that area there. David didn't want the land. He gave it to James and James came up here and established himself a store in Aaronsburg in the early years before the town was settled."

I ask if the James Duncan family is still here.

"No. There aren't really any early families around other than Stovers. A lot of them! Just look in the phone book."

Opposite Page: Section of 1796 map of The State of Pennsylvania. Aaronsburg is shown at the center of the map's left edge with the predecessor for Route 45 starting at Aaronsburg, running east and passing north of Penns Creek and Northumberland. Carlisle is shown to the left of Harrisburg at center bottom, and Lancaster at the lower right. Azilum was south of Tyoga Point at the map's top. Courtesy of Carnegie Library of Pittsburgh.

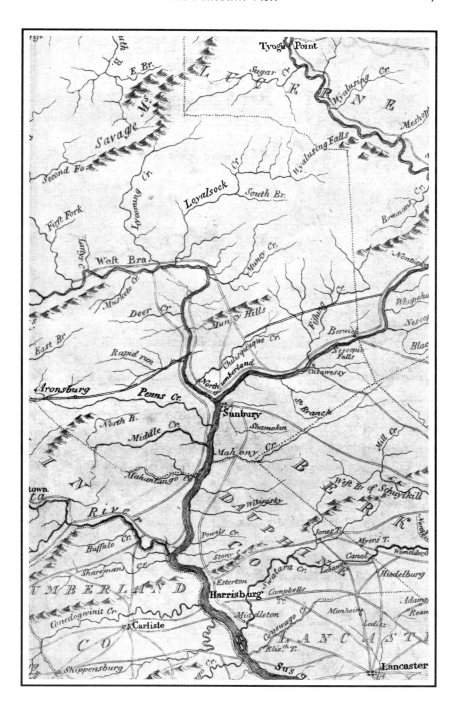

As we take a breather and sit for a while around the book-laden table that totally fills his cramped office partition, Bruce convinces me that Aaronsburg had no practical reason to exist. It was a purely political creation. Every other town in Penns Valley had a creek as its economic foundation, a water source for powering the mills to support industry, and hinted at water in its name: Millheim, Spring Mills, and Liberty Mills, now called Woodward.

As the state expanded westward, it was important to have as a capital a central location that was equally accessible for everybody to transact state business. Speaking of Aaron Levy's plan, Bruce says, "It's an 18th-century Levittown, and he was the Bill Levitt of his day. He plops his grid down in the middle of nowhere and says we're going to have a state capital here because the state capital at Philadelphia down at the confluence of the Delaware and the Schuylkill Rivers is essentially a swamp ."

"Philadelphia also happened to be the seat of government of the entire country at the time ," I interject while Bruce continues without pause. "So Levy says, 'Hey, I've got this 300 acres of land that was owned by Alexander Grant here in the middle of the state, roughly the geographic center of the state. We'll found a town here.' "

Grant was the soldier who owned and sold the tract. There were other tracts throughout the valley. Some soldiers did come up and stake their claims, but most of them sold. Aaronsburg was laid out in a typical 18th century town plan.

"If the town had devolved the way Levy had planned it we'd all have these long quarter-acre lots. We'd look a lot like Mifflinburg." Mifflinburg is a town in Union County, east of Aaronsburg over the Narrows, a high densely wooded area that separates the eastern, Susquehanna Valley part of Route 45 from Penns Valley to the west. Mifflinburg was next on my list to explore.

Bruce is indefatigable. We move on.

"Now, figure out what this is?" He hands me a strange brass object.

"Is it an oil can?" I question.

"No! It should talk to you. You look for the design a lot of the time. That'll tell you something. It's not a crank. It doesn't turn. You think maybe it's a pipe?"

"It's got a hole that goes right through!"

"So this is where it fits," sticking one end of it in his ear.

"A hearing aid. Right!" We laugh together.

"Now, these documents over here," he points to a wall hung with glassine-encased fragile-looking papers, "what was happening was that the town was never really going to take off as the state capital. Harrisburg was the logical choice because you have water, a water route. Aaronsburg doesn't. Now these three documents tell me what was happening here. In 1797 Michael Weaver was listed as a shopkeeper. He buys lot number 123 from Aaron Levy for 15 pounds. This deed is on vellum parchment, a dried animal skin, highly taxed and expensive to make. You don't want to waste these things. Why do you have this funny margin cut and where do you get the term indenture? Well, you cut the piece up like a jigsaw puzzle. The buyer and seller at the courthouse each need a copy of the documents. No copy machines. So he cut the thing up like a jigsaw puzzle so if there's any chance of a border dispute later on down the road, you can fit the pieces back together. That's also how they got the term for high school or college diplomas - a sheepskin." I am whipsawed by Bruce's tumbling thoughts that have led us back to dead animals.

"Another thing is the paper. After the area became more civilized, more settled, you don't see the vellum parchment; you see paper. Because paper's now being brought up from areas like Harrisburg. Up until 1850, you needed a large population to make paper because it's made out of recycled rags. You needed a ragpicker to go around. Feel the difference in that." I can feel what he means in its texture and pliancy. Bruce continues on. "This is the paper we use today. I can tell just by the feel of the paper that this is before 1850, that's after 1850, because this is recycled rags. And after 1850 it's wood pulp. There's more acid involved in manufacture of the modern paper and so it presents a problem for conservation."

"Getting back to Weaver?" I try to keep him on track.

"He's listed as a shopkeeper. He buys that lot. Eleven years later he's selling it in 1808 to Philip Moore. Weaver's now listed as an innkeeper and Moore's listed as a farmer. What's going on? He wants to get in on the action. The price has gone up from 15 pounds to 170 pounds in only 11 years time. That means that there's now a structure on the property and what Weaver's doing is providing lodging for people. If you're on the road sloggin' along at ten miles a day, the lights of civilization are sure lookin' good. If you look on this map back here, Aaronsburg is the only town in 1796 this far north and west between Sunbury and

Pittsburgh. That's a distance of at least 180 miles! That's what these people are doing—providing lodging."

On close examination, this large reproduction map, dated MDCCX-CII and dedicated to Governor Thomas Mifflin by its creator Reading Howell, shows Aaronsburg with a small cluster of "dwelling houses" on an existing road which roughly follows today's Route 45. Some of the symbols in this 1796 map's legend are A Bridle Road or Horse Path, An Indian Town, A House of Worship, A Furnace, A Forge, A Grist Mill, A Saw Mill, An Indian Path, A Water which Sinks, and Minerals. Almost a minimalist's poem of settler life.

"Now, this here is a credit voucher from the town of Woodward," he hands me a small piece of paper enclosed in glassine. "Every little town had a bank up until the Federal Reserve brought them all together in 1913. You had these little independent banks. Now the Motz family has a racket going. They have the Woodward Inn, they have the bank, they have the mill, they have the store and they own all the land above town so that a lot of lumbering interests are involved as well. By having the store and the gristmill, all the farmers bring them their grain. They have a credit economy. This is a credit voucher for five cents . . . in 1862. Motz's Bank. The house is still there in Woodward. That's the only other town in Haines Township at the end of the county, east of here. Now you have 20 of these vouchers, which you present, at the store, Motz's store, and you'll get five dollars in gold when you present them.

"In 1877, that's 15 years later, he's moved to Millheim. Millheim's where the action is because the railroad has come through. And Millheim has now eclipsed Aaronsburg and Woodward as the economic

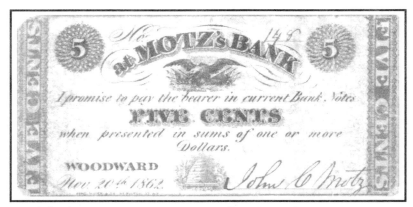

Motz's bank currency. Courtesy Penns Valley Historical Association.

center of Penns Valley. It's at a crossroads. On your way here from Pittsburgh you probably passed the only red light in the center of the valley. That's the crossroads accommodating all the produce that comes out of Brush Valley. So Motz moved the bank to Millheim in 1877. By 1884 it is now the Millheim Banking Company. But you know he's still running the show because he has advertising in the margin of his checks.

"Moving along here you see we're still paying in gold and silver specie, in hard cash. You're not paying by check or by credit card. So it's hard cash. There was so much gold accumulated in this town that in 1810, by the time they started the Centre Bank in Bellefonte, they needed two wagon loads to haul all the gold up to Bellefonte. So you see there was quite a bit of jack in this town."

With an unspoken "ta da" and a smile Bruce hands me a document he plucks off a moveable wall panel that is covered with other glassine encased papers.

"This is my all time favorite item in the entire museum. It's an article of agreement between William Hoover, Walker Township, and Jacob Stover. Stover lived right next door to my place where the coal yard is now. He had a tannery. Here's his signature, here's Hoover's. See, that's a mark. That means he could not read or write his own name. So we know a little bit about those two individuals. Hoover agrees in this article of agreement to sell his rights, titles and claims of Alice for 50 dollars."

"Of what?"

"Of Alice. But we don't know who or what is Alice. Cow? Pig? Wife? Daughter? Right! You're playing detective. This was 1824. Now," handing me another paper, "this is two years earlier, the Jacob Hubler estate sale. Hubler's kicked the bucket. They're selling off all his worldly goods. You find things like a plow going for 25 cents, an iron kettle going for $3.40. That tells me the plow was probably made out of wood. Then you get to the animals. There's a choice hog going for $3.75; red cow, white face, $7.50; a bull, $9.75. Now, that's a description of an animal. A bull is your most expensive farm animal. He's gone for almost ten bucks. He can do one thing and he does it well. But Alice is going for 50 bucks, five times as much. That means she can do a lot of different things. So she probably is a human being."

"A slave?"

"The tip-off is, you don't see Elsie, the cow. This just has Alice on

Alice bill of sale. Courtesy Penns Valley Historical Association.

it. Now is Alice white or is she black?   If she was white she might be an indentured servant. But that institution was pretty much out of the system by 1824. The other tip-off is that white people have last names. And Alice has no last name!   Now the problem we have with this is, Pennsylvania was the first state to emancipate slaves in 1780 and here we have 1824. What gives?   In 1780, if you were black and were born in 1780 or after, you would be automatically free. If you were born before 1780 you'll have to wait at least 47 years until you are automatically free, unless ole Massa frees you. Why?   The 50 dollars she's being bought and sold for. We can draw from this how old she is. She has to be at least 44 years old . . . from 1780 to 1824. That's prime mammy age and she's going for 50 dollars. That would translate today to about $2,500. Now would you appreciate the government wiping out a $2,500 invest-ment overnight with the stroke of a pen by freeing your slaves? No! The whole thing is economics!   It had nothing to do with morality in this case, unfortunately. This is next to an animal. It's not a human being as we know it—legally." He points to another article. "Here's a young girl named Margaret Swartz."

"So that's the end of Alice," I sigh?

"Pretty much. It's just a hunch, though. I can theorize."

I'm left hanging and a little frustrated.

"This young girl named Margaret Swartz," he continues unabashed, "she's 14 years old. Father passed away. Mom ships her out to work. This is a legal contract she enters into as an apprenticeship to learn to be a housewife. She has a four-year contract. She'll get her sewing, her spinning, her religion, her German language, her room and board. At the end of her four-year term she gets a bed-set, bed and bedding, the value of 25 dollars. That's quite a bit. And one good cow!

"A good cow?"

"Not a bad one, plus a chest and a spinning wheel. In the event she never marries, and she becomes a spinster, that's how we get the term, she'll still be able to provide for herself . . . that spinning wheel. But, she's gonna be a good catch! We aren't talking looks here. We're talking practicality. We're talking Germanic here. This young fella over here took three years to become a tanner, and here, two years to become a carpenter. But four years to become a housewife? So you can see how important her skills are gonna be in this society."

"Or maybe they may be taking advantage of her," I hypothesize?

"We don't know that. As I was telling you about things talking to you, this is a flax break." He holds up a wood and metal contraption. "How was I able to determine that? The lady upstairs who donated it said her son bought it at a sale, but they didn't know what it was. Hoped I could tell her. 'Okay, well,' I said, 'this stuff talks to you. Want to try to identify something? The legs are spindly so you know it can't take a lot of stress. Look at the iron. You get an idea it's from about 1820 from the nails and the crudity of the iron. It's a flat surface squared off. It's not sharp, so it's not cutting something. It's chopping or breaking apart something, which would have to be a vegetable fiber. And flax would be it, so you could break it there and pull the fiber out to make linen."

Bruce is pleased with his logical deduction. He obviously enjoys the detective work.

"To give you an idea about the traveling conditions . . . this is a letter a fellow wrote in 1818. He was riding his horse from Lewisburg to

Lewistown. He got as far as past Middleburg, which was probably called Swinesburg Town at the time, and his horse got stuck in the flood. He had to turn around and come back and couldn't make a session at court. That's what this letter's about. This will give you an idea what the roads were like. They were not very dependable. And at that time of the year, March, it means the spring freshet, the flood."

It's amazing to see the amount of stuff Bruce has crammed into this small basement. And apparently some purists protest at what they consider his indiscriminate, open-handed acceptance of new acquisitions. Hanging from the low ceiling are some blue and beige homespun coverlets. Teeple tells me that Emanuel Ettinger wove them in Jacquard patterns from about 1835 to about 1865.

Bruce continues. "As I was saying, Aaronsburg was the economic center of the valley up until the Civil War and the railroad. You had a lot of cottage industries. Didn't require much water. These Jacquard designs, too, they exchanged the cards, the patterning cards, among each other. You'll see a lot of similarity between this pattern and the guy down in Pine Grove Mills, 35 or 40 miles away. Like computer cards, that's what they were. That's probably how those computer whizzes got the idea, from using these cards. The cards with punched out designs were originally attached to a loom, which then was guided automatically to create inwoven patterns."

"A fella named Michael Bollinger was making furniture around here at the time, too. Here's a power lathe and jigsaw like his. And these are some shoes made by a fella named Henry Steffen who lived across the street. That house has since been torn down." Fingering the tools he remarks that people in town up until the 1940s and 50s were still using them to repair their own shoes.

"Was the original population all German?" I ask.

"No, there were a lot of Scotch-Irish here, too. But for the most part they were German. The language they spoke was mainly Pennsylvania Dutch. German farming techniques were developed in limestone valleys just like around here. Scotch-Irish liked to farm shale soils because that's what they were used to back home in the old country. That's why they moved on. You tended to farm areas you were accustomed to.

"Stover's store, right there at the Texaco sign here in Aaronsburg, has been a store since 1802. There was a Polish refugee named Lyons Mussina who's buried up at the Reformed cemetery, he had that store." He clarifies that this wasn't the Duncan store.

I think to myself, is Mussina a refugee because he is Polish, while the Scotch-Irish and Germans are considered settlers? Looking at a store ledger from 1826, Bruce, rushing on giving me no time to ponder, points out how people were spending their money then.

"Today you go out and buy a can of beans. Back then you buy things that are imported like sugar—maybe flour. But the flour you would have yourself, more than likely, or would get it from a nearby mill. Now, for recycling. Indians were recycling their spearpoints and arrowheads over and over again because it's a big investment in time and effort. That's about two hours work to make a spearpoint, so you're gonna recycle that thing as much as you can. Material. These settlers are recycling cloth after it's been used up as clothing. That's one of the things you would have bought here at the store. You recycle it into a quilt. The whole notion of *not* recycling is what's new today."

I read from the ledger, "Rosin, coffee, chocolate, files? . . . "

"Now sugar . . . a pound of sugar is 14 cents. That sounds cheap. Let me translate that. Until Henry Ford invented the eight-hour workday, you worked ten hours a day. You were paid ten cents an hour or a dollar a day. That's the prevailing wage rate for a day laborer. At 14 cents, that would be roughly an hour and a half's work. What's an hour and a half's wage today? A day laborer makes about six or seven dollars an hour. So now we're talking nine, ten or twelve dollars a pound for sugar!"

I break in again, emboldened by our more relaxed give and take. "Now here we've got a pint of whiskey, nails, butter."

The nails, he tells me, might have been brought into the area or the metal, and the local blacksmith might have made them.

"Butter's a surprise—because you'd think that—" I practically sputter.

"Well, if you lived in town you might not have a cow," Bruce retorts.

I notice in a ledger entry that the same person gets the whiskey and tobacco. It's Barbara Mussina, wife or daughter of the store owner. You get a small inkling of people's priorities by what they buy.

"Now the year is 1826 so this would be rag," I deduce, pointing to the ledger and remembering his lesson.

"And this," handing me a newspaper, "is 1850. You feel the difference. Wood pulp paper would not be feeling like that. A lot cheesier quality."

He has so much more he wants to show and tell. Stereopticon slides from the 1880s, uniforms and record books from marching bands from Aaronsburg, Coburn and Millheim, food ration points and stamps from World War II, gas masks, an old pump organ from Paradise church, a map of the then United States from 1843 with no Oklahoma, Texas, Kansas, Iowa, Wisconsin or West Virginia, an 1874 washing machine, a 1909 non-electrified Alka vacuum cleaner, a left-handed sickle. Too much to deal with all at once.

Undaunted he continues.

"This is the local militia muster list from the War of 1812. This fella for example, the captain of the company, he gets a political commission from some friends down in Harrisburg. They were gonna go fight Redcoats. So he rounds up a bunch of people to help out. There's a wide range of ages from 14 to 50. The older fella is probably the town drunk who wants to make a few extra bucks. Nothing else to do. He doesn't have a farm or a family to tie him down. You find things listed as public property or GI. But you don't see rifles. They're all private property. Now, if you're gonna go off to fight Redcoats, are you gonna take old trusty Betsy, your squirrel rifle that you know and love so well, or are you gonna take a gun you know nothing about? You're gonna take old trusty Betsy. Sure enough. That's private property here. This is a militia tax record. We didn't have a standing army like we have today. You had these local informal militias.

"Come on out here," he summons me to a bookcase in the back room. "I'll show you a few last minute things. If you've got an ancestor who came over here on a boat, these volumes will tell you what boat they came in on, what day they came—the whole works. That is, if you are of German descent. The funny thing is—in the mid 1700s you have a lot of people like Ben Franklin saying 'you've got all these Germans coming and taking our jobs.' Sounds familiar, doesn't it? The Italians, the Irish? Now it's the Mexicans—they're all takin' our jobs. It's the same bitch they had about the Germans.

"Now this is the last thing, pointing at a wall with old newspaper clippings, it's the Aaronsburg Story. I know you've heard about it."

I nod. There's a book I'd been reading by Arthur Lewis called *The Aaronsburg Story* which details the creation of a pageant in 1949 commemorating the 150th anniversary of an event surrounding an ecumenical gesture by Aaron Levy, founder of the town.

"The whole notion of being a good neighbor is essentially what that was all about. Token movie star, Cornel Wilde, Justice Frankfurter, Ralph Bunche of the UN, Daniel Poling was the Billy Graham of his day, Wild Bill Donovan from the OSS."

Reading the newspaper article aloud I question, "Two thousand at the most were expected to attend and 30,000 did? Somewhere I read 56,000."

"There was a fellow there from Penn State who estimated crowds for the football team and he said anywhere from 30,000 to 50,000. Anyway, it was a good size crowd. That was the town's day in the sun. And the thing that got me was that this was a recurring theme of redemption. You had Aaron Levy here and he was hoarding salt and he gives this pewter communion set. I mean, this blows everybody's ecumenical mind. It's 1949! What's this Jew 200 years ago doing this type of thing?"

I gulp and ask, "Where is the pewter communion set today? Here in the museum?"

Bruce shakes his head no, and with a rueful expression says, "It should be. There's a fella named Ralph Musick, I think he has it. At his house, if they're not keeping it up at the church. There's a whole Aaronsburg cult. Politics." He lets the rest of the phrase dangle in the air.

"Can we talk about that another time?" I suggest wearily, hopefully.

"Another time, yeah," he answers. "It's a real howl. It can be a pain in the neck. No, it's a fascinating town. Really is. Quirky history. It's a lot of fun. I really enjoy the people. This is a volunteer job, you know. This is a hobby."

"Well, this is a great start . . . a really great start," I thank him.

"Take one of these with you if you like," handing me a brochure. "They have the phone number in the back and the hours," he says as we climb back out into the quiet autumn twilight.

As I head back to my car, my head spinning, I think, "Yep—great start—and a long road ahead."

Chapter 2

THE ROAD: HISTORY & GEOGRAPHY

On a fair Spring day in 1949, says Arthur Lewis in *The Aaronsburg Story*, while driving west along Route 45 from the town of Jim Thorpe, Carbon County, Pennsylvania, en route to his home in Pittsburgh, he spotted a modest historic marker at the edge of the village of Aaronsburg. Checking current Pennsylvania road maps to retrace his route, I see that is not where one finds Route 45 today. A map of 1949 shows that a route designated as 45 did indeed go that far east. But today Route 45 starts at an abrupt right angle near Mooresdale in Montour County, some 30 odd miles west of Jim Thorpe. Near Mooresdale, not through it as it once did. And it dead ends abruptly, "not with a bang, but a whimper," at the village of Water Street in Huntingdon County, 100 miles to the West, in the process traversing five counties.

The designation, Route 45, is merely PennDot's number bestowed on it in the last 50 years. Originally it was simply called the Turnpike. Route designations and contours change frequently with time for many reasons: to straighten a rough curve, accommodate an irate landowner, or circumvent an over-trafficked village. The map in central Pennsylvania is dotted with place names, places once-upon-a-time important enough to name, but today forgotten. What remains is a single farmstead or an abandoned cemetery or a noble maple, where once there was a small village or family enclave.

In Union County along Route 45, I came across an empty but restored one-room octagonal stone schoolhouse, which the historic marker called Sodom. No one knows why it was weighted with that ominous Biblical name. No salt hoarders in sight. There wasn't a trace of other buildings nearby. I've paced the area looking for old foundations or burned brick chimneys, any hint of former habitation, without success. But back in 1843, Charles Trego, in *A Geography of Pennsylvania*, describes Sodom as "a post village on Chilisquaque Creek, seven miles north of Sunbury," containing "twelve or fifteen houses, a store and a tavern." Just as in Rome, where ancient ruins like the Coliseum have been scavenged for the stone and bricks of Renaissance buildings, so too have traces of early settlements along Pennsylvania roads disappeared, only to be found incorporated in a nearby house or barn foundation.

Back in the 18th century, these country roads were, in reality, dirt tracks. Sometimes winter snows made them impassable by horse and wagon. The one exception was when the terrain froze smooth in winter, allowing sleighs to fly over snow-flattened ruts. The horses could even cross streams on solid ice. Following the natural contours of the land, many of the roads were originally trails blazed by Indians in pursuit of game or fish or salt or seasonal wild produce. Says John Brinckerhoff Jackson in *A Sense of PLACE . . . a Sense of TIME*, "When woodland eastern America was invaded by colonists from England and France, the paths created by the Indian farmers and hunters were taken over by the newcomers and used as they had used paths and lanes of the home-

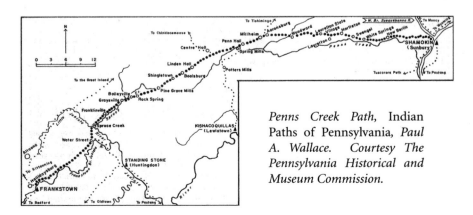

Penns Creek Path, Indian Paths of Pennsylvania, *Paul A. Wallace. Courtesy The Pennsylvania Historical and Museum Commission.*

land. Finally the paths became crude roads for carts and wagons and horsemen, less and less traveled by Indians." The single animal spoor and narrow Indian trail was widened through use by early eastern buffalo herds, then by wagons riding abreast. Various entrepreneurs built up sections of roads through their own land. Eventually these sections were connected into a turnpike with tollhouses introduced to help recoup costs.

The first toll road in Centre County went from Sunbury to Aaronsburg, the route Aaron Levy took to reach his land in the 1780s. It started at Blue Hill across the Susquehanna River from his home in Northumberland, followed Chief Shikellamy's Penns Creek Path, and angled up through New Berlin and White Springs, joining the present Route 45 at Hartleton.   It continued across the seven-mile Narrows to Woodward. This was the private road Reuben Haines, the Quaker brewer from Philadelphia, built in 1766 to gain access to the 12,000 acres he owned as far west as Spring Mills. From there on, a road built by General James Potter continues west.

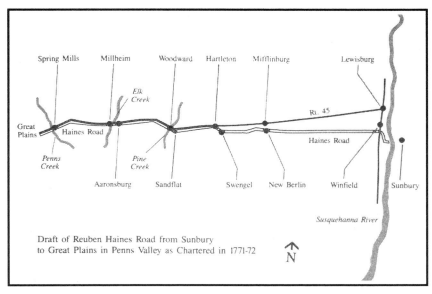

Haines Road paralleled the current Route 45 through lower Penns Valley, diverging only at Woodward.   This was Aaron Levy's route to what became Aaronsburg. Millheim, Millheim Bicentennial Magazine, p. 10, 1988, Courtesy of Penns Valley Historical Association.

Tollgate keepers were given free housing to move the pole aside after appropriate fees were paid. Typical fees were:

A score of sheep.. 4 cents
A score of hogs .... 6 cents
A score of cattle... 12 cents
Every horse or mule laden or unladen, with rider or led...... 3 cents
A 2-wheeled vehicle drawn by 1 horse.................................... 6 cents
A 2-wheeled vehicle drawn by 2 horses .... 9 cents
A 4-wheeled vehicle drawn by 2 horses .... 12 cents
A 4-wheeled vehicle drawn by 4 horses .... 20 cents
A sled or sleigh for each horse... 2 cents

A few of these tollhouses still exist. Helen Fahy, former president of the Penns Valley Conservation Association, lives in one on Route 45 near Spring Mills.

Still later, the county or state took charge and built bridges over rivers and ravines. In the 20th century, once properly surfaced, these country roads were passable throughout the year. In my wanderings I met a woman whose husband owns a combination barber/ammo shop. She remembers when her father was on a work gang, paving Route 45 for the first time for 25 cents an hour. That was in the 1930s.

It was Potter who first discovered Penns Valley in 1764, coming at it from the north. Upon reaching the crest of Nittany Mountain, thrilled at the remote, peaceful valley below, he exclaimed to his aide, "By heavens, Thompson, I have discovered an empire!" On his return to Philadelphia, Potter promptly applied for a patent to the land, only to discover that Haines already had taken title. Together they divided the tract, Haines, the English Quaker, taking the eastern half of the valley; Potter, the Scotch Presbyterian, the west. It was Haines who shrewdly created a transportation monopoly at the forks of the Susquehanna River separating the towns of Sunbury and Northumberland. He acquired land along the river's edge and, at the same time, the right to operate a ferry gaining access control to his road and his land. Today the names Potter Township and Haines Township attest to the original proprietorship that takes up most of the area of present-day eastern Centre County.

As Bruce Teeple told me, the unusual land configuration of this region may be due to the continent of Africa nudging what is now the coastal area around Delaware, at one point in geologic time. The term "anticlinorum" is used to describe the bending and buckling of the earth's surface. I learned from Peirce Lewis to identify sedimentary sequences, large upfolded areas with repeated cycles of marine sediments, deposited when the area was part of an ocean. Route 45 is a ridge valley composed of limestone, shale, sandstone and conglomerate with some glacial debris called till, making the soil particularly good for farming. So good, in fact, that at some places topsoil reaches the remarkable depth of 15 feet. Sherman Day, writing in 1843, calls it "exuberant fertility." Along most of the way on either side are low sheltering hills.

When questioning geologists, I wanted to know when and how my road started. I speculated that it might have progressed from animal tracks to Indian paths to hunters' trails to wagon roads, as had many early roads. But no, except for human assistance over a mountainous section called the Narrows that run from Woodward to Laurelton, it was a naturally evolved configuration. The topography follows the structure of the stone that has eroded at different rates over the years. And limestone happens to last longer. It was the animals and man who followed nature's path here.

Route 45 can be divided roughly into three parts: two valleys that are separated by the Narrows. The latter is a belt of sandstone uplands about 15 miles long, all wooded, state forestland where hardly anyone ever lived, and nobody lives today. The Narrows was lumbered extensively in the past by transients, but never settled.

At its southwestern terminus at the village of Water Street, Route 45 winds through a confined limestone valley. The floor of the valley is limestone or shale, and the walls are sandstone ridges about 1,000 feet high. This part of the road was hard to reach, but once here, if a settler wanted to farm or to mine for iron on a small scale, this was a pretty good place to be. East from Water Street to Spring Mills, where the upland ridge begins, is known as Nittany Valley; and then, further east heading towards Woodward, as Penns Valley.

There is another unseen world along Route 45. This one is underground in the form of limestone caves. Edwin Valentine Mitchell, in *It's an Old Pennsylvania Custom*, goes so far as to claim, "In Centre County, it is said that you can go underground at one end of the county and emerge at the other end by threading your way through the natural subway formed by the series of caverns that underlie the region." No self-respecting speleologist will confirm this fantasy, according to Professors Elizabeth and William White of State College. However, the dissolution of limestone by water over eons has created a tasty Swiss cheese of explorable caves in the region, over 70 named and investigated in Centre County alone. Some, like Indian Cave, Penns Cave and Woodward Cave have become commercial tourist attractions. Formations of stalactites and stalagmites and flowstone sport fanciful names. And each place has its legend of a lost Indian maiden, unrequited lovers, sheltered bandits, or, more recently, wildly abandoned teenage revelers. By far the largest and most impressive, according to knowledgeable cavers, is Hosterman's Pit, which is now off-limits and possibly destroyed, since it is part of a limestone mining operation near Aaronsburg.

Buffalo Valley in the Susquehanna Valley region is on the eastern side of the Narrows.

By 1830, there was nothing more to attract new people to the eastern and western ends of the road. All the agricultural land was taken, and the towns along the way had ceased to grow. The iron industry gave both ends a shot in the arm from about 1830 to 1900. Then, having exhausted the wood for charcoal, and with the ore difficult to extract, the industry moved west to Pittsburgh.

Since then, the two areas of growth to which outsiders have been drawn are focused not on farming or mining, but on higher education: Bucknell University in Lewisburg in the east in Buffalo Valley, and Penn State at State College in the west in Nittany Valley. The latter, by far the larger, has had the greater impact for change on the area. Its urbanizing tentacles have encroached on the land in ever widening circles. Once there were widespread self-contained clusters of farms, dominated by soaring silos and imposing forebay barns with compatible spring houses, pole buildings, corn cribs, horse, cow and wagon sheds nestling near the old family Georgian farmhouse of brick or mountain stone. Now suburban-style housing developments have sprung up in their place. Bare of stands of trees, a crop of architecturally mongrelized opulent single-family homes have sprouted like dragon's teeth across the undulating open former farmland. The view to me was a visceral kick in the gut calling up imagery from another time and place. They resemble the lone juvenile male wildebeests I saw on the open windy plains of Kenya, confined and waiting forlornly within the territory they had defined by spraying urine, hoping to entice a passing stray female. These homeowners, though, are just playing out one version of the American dream and some day, these nouveaux chateaux will have settled into the landscape and drawn to themselves their contemporary accretion of foundation plantings and tennis courts, swimming pools, pool houses, garden sheds and gazebos. Probably the Native Americans thought something similar at the arrival of the original European settlers who encroached and despoiled at will. I sorely wish that the Amish, who respect and farm the remaining land, would somehow manage to stem the invasion.

The present Route 45, which traverses the five counties of Huntingdon, Centre, Union, Northumberland, and Mon tour, and covers about 100 miles, retains a feel of the old 19th-century definition of road: "a passage between two places, wide and level enough to accommodate vehicles as well as horses and persons traveling on foot." Today, one drives through a valley of rolling farmland fringed with, and enclosed by, low mountains. Many of the German Georgian farmhouses of wood, brick or mountain stone are set far back off the road, flanked by buggy sheds and well houses. Outscaled red barns, some with aluminum-domed silos standing at attention, dwarf them.

A style of barn particular to this region of Pennsylvania, and brought from the Palatine by the early German settlers is called a bank or forebay barn (from the German *vorbei*). Typically, it has a southward orientation nestled into a bank, an early solar device that permits the low-lying winter sun to heat the stables. The north side has a cantilevered overhang that affords shade for cattle in summer, and protection for cordwood from the elements. Frequently, these forebay barns are ennobled with Gothic pointed windows resembling nearby Gothic revival churches. No matter how often I have asked, I have been unable to find out why these pragmatic farmers took the trouble to add the uplifting spiritual flourish to a barn. The most satisfying answer is that very likely the church and barn builder was the same carpenter, using the same pocket-sized stylebook for inspiration. In Victorian times, when many of these barns were built, it was a matter of a farmer's pride to outdo and impress his neighbor by having the largest barn, decorated with the most elaborate architectural details.

Curiously, none of the farmhouses have these features. They maintain their 18th and 19th century simplicity, leaving one to ponder what the farmer considered more important. Did he equate his barn with his church? Jeff Wert, a local historian, quotes a Confederate officer:

Forebay Barn with German Gothic influences.　Photo by Joan Morse Gordon.

"Pennsylvanians are decidedly people of barns, not brains." Wert claims that his father-in-law, Ralph Long, who farmed for over 40 years, said he would rather, if push came to shove, have his farmhouse burn down. And what did Mrs. Long, the farmer's wife have, if anything, to say about it?

A survey ordered by President Thomas Jefferson in 1785 divided all the land to the west, at the juncture of the Pennsylvania, West Virginia, Ohio territories, into grids, ignoring land contour and natural phenomena. My road, fortunately located further east, follows its own natural, graceful way, bordering creeks, centered in its valleys, with unexpected striking vistas ahead over its next gentle hill. Back in the 18th century, it was thought that this road, too, would continue west. But with the arrival of the railroads and canals, more efficient means of transport, Route 45 became, and has remained, a little used byway for more than 100 years.

Church with German Gothic influences. Photo by Joan Morse Gordon.

Chapter 3

WILLIAM PENN, FOUNDER

W ho were the inhabitants of this region? How did they arrive? What factors brought them? And what circumstances convinced them to stay or move on?

Native Americans in the New World for thousands of years had hunted and gathered and named and used the land freely without the remotest concept of personal ownership, or the need for ownership. The vast American landscape was collectively theirs to use for as long as they remembered. All the way back to their mythic past 15,000 years ago, they believed their ancestors emerged from a deep cavern underground, vaguely somewhere in the far west of this continent, and roamed and lived off the land without thought or qualm. Scientists, though, speculate they had migrated overland from Asia at a time when the Asian landmass adjoined Alaska over the shallow Bering Strait. Even this theory is in question today. Our first Americans, Upper Paleolithic hunters and gatherers, spread first southward along the Pacific coast, and later eastward across the continent, adapting their lives to the circumstances of their diverse environments.

The Leni Lenape, or Delaware Indians, are believed to have lived in the Pennsylvania area as early as the 11th century BC. Over time they modified their nomadic ways, creating stable villages and planting crops, but keeping their animistic religious beliefs, always with the idea of using, not owning, the land. Relics of their way of life rest today in a cabinet in the Penns Valley Historical Association in Aaronsburg, PA.

With the invasion of European settlers much later, the wanderings of North American Indians had been systematically stilled and obliterated under western man's treaties and land grants. European settlers arrived by the boatload and staked out their own specific land claims, thus consigning the American Indians' boundaryless world into oblivion.

In a sense, William Penn was a bridge between these native Americans and later patterns of European settlement.

William Penn was born at Tower Hill, London on October 15, 1644, and started early in life as a rebel and an embarrassment to his family. Penn entered Oxford University at 15, and soon came under the influence of Thomas Loe, a Quaker minister. Adhering to Quaker tradition, not the dicta of the Church of England, his family's religious tradition, he refused to attend chapel or wear the required gown. He was soon expelled for stripping others of their gowns. This incensed his father, Sir William Penn, a distinguished naval officer. By the time his son was ten and he 33, Sir William was made General of the Sea and given an extravagant chain of gold. Absent at sea for months at a time, he was a father-hero to worship, but from afar. Since no other school under the dominion of the Church of England would accept his son, despite the intercession of diarist Samuel Pepys who searched for a school for "difficult youth," Sir William ordered the miscreant out of his house. However, Mrs. Penn interceded on behalf of her son, and he was sent on a grand tour of the continent at the age of 17.

Three years later, in 1664, Mrs. Pepys informs her husband, "Mr. Pen, Sir William's son, is come back from France—a most modish person, grown, she says, a fine gentleman." A few weeks later, after dining with the Penns, Pepys notes the younger Penn's "French garb and affected manner of speech and gait. I fear all real profit he hath made of his travel will signify little." The following year his father sent him to Ireland to manage the family estate. Once again, young Penn fell under the influence of Thomas Loe, and, in December 1667, Pepys records a friend telling him, "Mr. William Pen, who is lately come of Ireland, is a Quaker again, or some very melancholy thing." This time the young man was fully committed to the Quaker faith, flouting his family's close affiliation with the Crown by writing diatribes against Papists, Protestants, the Church of England and the Separatists . . . dissenters other than Quakers. He wrote one incendiary pamphlet, *The Sandy Foundation Shaken*, which questioned the Holy Trinity. This was the last straw, according to the Bishop of London, who claimed Penn hadn't submitted the manuscript in advance of publication to be checked by the censor. His punishment: 8 months and 16 days in the Tower of London, with no trial. Penn was unrepentant.

Two weeks before his father's death in 1670, Penn and William Mead, a linen-draper, were brought to trial at the Old Bailey for preaching in Gracechurch Street "to the great disturbance of the King's peace," thus violating the Conventicle Act, a law prohibiting dissenters' religious gatherings. During the trial, Penn kept his hat on, a custom of Quakers who would not remove their hats even in the presence of kings. He was considered a "smug and troublesome fellow." Since they was being tried on the basis of the Common Law, by its nature unwritten, Penn insisted perversely on seeing a copy. The jury freed Mead. Speaking in his own defense Penn declared, "If William Mead be Not Guilty, it consequently follows, that I am clear, since you have indicted us of a Conspiracy, and I could not conspire alone." The jury, holding out against the tribunal's decision, despite being locked up and denied food, drink or heat for two nights, found Penn guilty of speaking subversively, but refused to find him guilty of unlawful assembly. This proved to be a landmark case after which juries' rights were clarified. In the process, Penn became a hero because of his outspoken advocacy of civil rights. His father quietly paid his fine so that two weeks later when his father died Penn was free to mourn together with his family at the time of the Admiral's death. Left with a comfortable legacy, Penn spent the next several years traveling, preaching, writing and settling into marriage, procreation, and moderate Quaker ways.

In 1681, King Charles II granted William Penn a patent for a province in the new American colonies. This land grant was to repay a debt of 16,000 pounds owed by the Crown to the estate of Penn's father. Penn called his province "Sylvania," for its abundant woodlands. However, King Charles II changed the name to "Pennsylvania," or "Penns Woods," out of "regard to the memorie and meritts of Sir William Penn in divers services, and particularly his conduct, courage, and discretion unto our dearest brother, James, Duke of York, in that signal battle and victory fought and obtained against the Dutch . . . 1665." Historians report that Sir William kept secret certain embarrassing mistakes of his patron, the Duke of York.

Pennsylvania covered a wide expanse, all the way from the Delaware to the Ohio River, a distance of over 300 miles. And it abutted Maryland and the territory known as the Jerseys, with slightly fuzzy borders. This was territory that King Charles gave to his brother, James, the Duke of York, who had the absolute right to disburse, after displacing Dutch rule, in a 1667 treaty concluding the Dutch wars. Arthur Pound in *The Penns of Pennsylvania and England* says, "the English surrendered Polaroon in the East Indies and gained New Netherland, so lightly did the Dutch value their continental American holdings as compared with the spice trade."

The landmass of Penn's new province made him the largest landholder in the New World. Pennsylvania was almost as large as all of England. In the charter for Pennsylvania, Penn was made "proprietary" and supreme governor, with the power to make laws "with advice, assent and approbation of the freemen, of appointing officers, and of granting pardons." The Crown reserved power in the areas of trade, commerce and taxation. Penn's sole obligation to the Crown for this feudal grant was an annual "quit-rent due the King of two beaver skins a year and one-fifth of all the gold and silver to be found in Pennsylvania." Quit rent was just a token. Its function was to show who was boss. Pennsylvania, which was called the "keystone" because of its central position among the 13 original American colonies, proved later on to be a "gold mine," not of gold, but of coal and iron and top grade Valentine limestone.

William Penn, as a practicing and vocal Quaker preacher, trained in the law, had been frequently arrested in England for his quiet, non-violent religious beliefs. Now, as "owner, proprietor and governor of his new province," Penn was delighted at the opportunity to freely assemble and worship with many of his Quaker brethren in the New World, without fear of imprisonment. The idea of migrating had been seriously considered long before Penn's bonanza. He had some previous experience helping to settle Quaker emigrants in neighboring West Jersey.

With the security of his ownership of the Province, he determined to establish in Pennsylvania a colony of refuge, not only for Quakers, but for other "Europeans oppressed by constant wars and poor economic conditions, and by religious and political persecution, people of all sects from England, Ireland, Scotland, Wales, Germany, Holland, France and Switzerland." Penn advertised for potential colonists, whom he called adventurers, "willing to work out their own salvation:" … "farmers, day laborers, carpenters, masons, smiths, weavers, tailors, tanners, shoemakers, shipwrights," . . . all were welcome. He took pains to inform the Dutch, Swedish and Finnish settlers who, for 100 years, since the 1580s, were already established in the province, not to worry " . . . you shall be governed by laws of your own making."

Early on, Penn recognized the affinity between English Quakers and some Anabaptist sects in southern Germany. They both were pacifist religious groups who refused to take oaths, whose simplicity of dress and speech set them apart from, and made them suspect to, many of their fellow citizens. The Anabaptists also differed from other Protestant sects by their insistence on adult baptism. The Thirty Years' War (1618-48) ravaged a constant battleground since Roman times, the fertile Palatinate, which encompassed parts of southwestern Germany and Switzerland. The inhabitants' security was precarious and their livelihoods uncertain. Farmers' lives were normally ruled by weather and the seasons. But now invading armies trampled crops, stole cattle and savaged their wives and daughters. They were pawns, subject to the whim of the current invader. In addition, the Treaty of Westphalia in 1688 upheld the medieval right of a ruler to determine the religion of its inhabitants, many of whom had embraced Protestantism during the Reformation. Even their fellow Protestants discriminated against others, Amish and Mennonites among them. To these downtrodden peasants, the prospect of a new world where they would be free to farm in peace and practice their chosen religion as their own masters, was more than tantalizing.

In 1681, shortly after his release from Newgate where Penn was imprisoned for refusing, as a Quaker, to take an oath of allegiance to the Crown, he made the first of two trips to both proselytize and convince the Palatines to migrate. He set about advertising and promoting his ideas of religious, economic and civil freedom to these potential colonists. Once he was actually proprietor, Penn visited them again and sent printed invitations that included his equitable financial terms. His attractive offer called for the sale of 5,000 acres for the price of 100 pounds, plus his annual quit-rent of one shilling per 100 acres. Penn also offered a yearly rental of up to 200 acres at a penny an acre for those lacking the capital to buy the land outright. This atypical and generous offer would permit the poor, who gained passage from Europe as indentured servants, to pay off their debts and eventually become landowners in their own right, literally a whole new lease on life. The result of his offer is to be found in a pamphlet, *A Further Account of the Province of Pennsylvania and Its Improvements*:

> *"We have had about ninety sail of ships with passengers since the beginning of '82, and not one vessel, designed to the province through God's mercy, hitherto miscarried. The estimate of the people may be thus made: eighty to each ship, which comes to seven thousand, two hundred persons. . . . The people are a collection of divers nations in Europe: as, French, Dutch, Germans, Swedes, Danes, Finns, Scotch-Irish, and English; and of the last equal to all the rest . . . "*

Penn's counsel to the emigrants: "Count on labor before a crop." In his consideration for the new settlers, Penn did not overlook the rights of the Delaware or Leni Lenape Indians, still inhabiting the territory. In November 1683, the "Great Treaty," was convened with the Delaware chief Tamanend, establishing fair methods of payment and compensation for their land. They agreed to "live in love as long as the sun gave light."

While William Penn was in charge, relations with the Indians were peaceful. He took the trouble to learn the Indian language and had the wisdom to follow their customs in his dealings with them. In a 1682 treaty with the Delawares, in which he purchased land along the Delaware River, the area bought encompassed "as far as a man can walk in a day and a half." It was understood that ownership of land depended on securing deeds from native inhabitants. Starting with Penn's purchase in 1682, and continuing through 1792, Indian lands were legitimately purchased to form the current borders of Pennsylvania.

In 1737, long after his father's departure, Penn's son, Thomas, used the same walking measure contorted by deceit to trick the Lenape out of their rightful land. In what was called the "Walking Purchase," the Lenape lost 1,200 square miles. Lenape Lappawinsoe protested, "The walkers should have walkt for a few miles and then sat down and smoakt a Pipe . . . and not kept upon the Run, Run, Run all Day." The Lenape at first had believed the treaties confirmed their willingness to share the land. Their Great Spirit, they believed, created land, as well as water and sunshine for everyone, a belief they shared with their Australian aboriginal cousins. William Penn's dream of equity in his Holy Experiment crumbled due to such deception, causing distrust and hostility between the Indians and settlers, eventually culminating in the slaughter of settlers in the Great Runaway of May 1778 that Bruce Teeple had so colorfully described to me.

Phototype of William Penn's Treaty with the Indians *by Benjamin West. Courtesy of The Darlington Memorial Library, University of Pittsburgh.*

Sixteen eighty-two, the year in which Penn built Pennsbury, his home on the Delaware River, was also the year Penn formulated the colony's first constitution called the *Frame of Government*. In it he specified the division of church and state, an inspiration for Thomas Jefferson 100 years later in the Bill of Rights.

Penn's colony, beyond the urban environment of Philadelphia, was composed primarily of farmers. Their ethnic makeup was more diverse than the original settlers in New England or the South. The colony developed into neither a plantation society of the South, nor village-based communities of the North, dominated by village green, church and Town Hall. According to the authors of *A Concise Historical Atlas of Pennsylvania*, it was the village, or township concept that Penn desired. Although egalitarian regarding the practice of religion, Penn nevertheless envisioned a hierarchical manorial order consisting of landed gentry supported by village artisans and farmers. He divided the land into 78 manors and sold it, before the general sale, to English "first purchasers," setting aside one-tenth of the land for the use of lords of the manor. Instead, the mainly German settlers, adhering to their own desires, dispersed and established single family, owner-operated farms with small towns functioning principally as supply bases. And this form of loose-knit community is what you still find in Centre and Union counties today.

After his return to England in 1684, prompted by legal problems with Lord Baltimore over still-disputed boundaries for which he had to appear in person, Penn stayed on in England, despite his good intentions, returning only once to Pennsylvania in 1699 for two years. While here, in 1701, he wrote the *Charter of Privileges*, in which he mandated the concept of freedom of worship. Years later, when the first Continental Congress met in the fall of 1774, Philadelphia, Penn's City of Brotherly Love, was the only city where all members could worship freely.

His successful recruitment of settlers notwithstanding, Penn was an ideologue, not a clever businessman. Even with the promise of the natural abundance of Penns Woods to dispense, he still lost money. Ongoing income he expected from the quit rents of early settlers never materialized. He found himself again in prison in England in 1701, this time as a debtor. By default, the Commonwealth of Pennsylvania fell heir to Penn's private domain, distributing land certificates to discharged members of the militia in lieu of worthless paper currency.

Penn's colony, primarily Philadelphia, carried on the basic tenets of the Quakers, remaining a haven for diverse seekers of asylum. But as time went by, as it spread out and diversified with other religious and political philosophies, primarily with pragmatic entrepreneurs who saw the need to bear arms, Quaker beliefs were marginalized and eventually compromised. What emerged was not quite Penn's dream, but a vitally new and strong polyglot America. It was also, as I learned during my journey, the basis for much of the history of the valleys I came to know along Route 45.

Chapter 4

Aaron Levy, Entrepreneur

One day in 1760, season unknown, 18-year-old Aaron Levy debarked at the port of Philadelphia after a two-month ship's crossing from his home in Amsterdam. These are the bare facts that we know about the future founder of Aaronsburg. I can only speculate on young Aaron's initial mixed feelings of trepidation and anticipation facing that voyage and what followed. Due to the loss or destruction of his papers, we know nothing of that momentous occasion and little of his family, save that his father was also an Aaron. Since he was named after his father, and, in the Jewish Ashkenazi tradition a child is not named after a living person, it may be assumed that his father died prior to his birth. We also know he had an older brother and two sisters. It is also possible that he was a Sephardic Jew whose family had spent over 250 years in the relative freedom and security of the Netherlands after the dispersion of the Jews from Spain during the Spanish Inquisition in the late 15th century. But certain prayer books, owned by a nephew who immigrated to Philadelphia 35 years later, are annotated in Yiddish, a language not used by the Sephardim. This led Dr. Sidney Fish, Aaron's biographer, to assume the Levy family had Eastern or Central European roots confirming probable Ashkenazi lineage.

Levy's motivation to emigrate alone, without family or friends, from the known to the unknown, may have been solely for the adventure and to seek his fortune. Holland at the time of his departure was not at war, nor was there pestilence or plague. Amsterdam was a long established and respected center of Jewish scholarship. "Still," as David Brener states in *The Jews of Lancaster, Pennsylvania*, "Jews came to America, often over strong objections of relatives and friends." Even though there was a relaxation of discrimination towards Jews in some European countries, they "still had to live under petty political disabilities. Among these were having to live in ghettos; wearing of badges; exclusion from honorific office, political rights and the owning of land; not being allowed to join craft guilds or attend schools and universities; exclusion from certain professions; prohibition from marrying; subjection to humiliating oaths and discriminatory taxation; and the restriction of inheritance from father to only one son." This matter-of-fact list of Brener's of "petty political disabilities" appears incredibly repressive to an American Jew today; but it was a yoke borne so long by European Jews that it was an unquestioned accepted burden.

In Levy's case his determination to migrate was not to avoid the extreme persecution or privation of imprisonment or loss of home experienced earlier by dissenters: William Penn and the Quakers in England, and the Germans and Swiss from the Palatine invited by Penn sought a haven 100 years earlier in the late 17th-century. In Levy's time it was other dissenters, such as Joseph Priestley, his future neighbor in Northumberland, who fled from religious persecution in England. Levy was not a dissenter; his religion was beyond the pale, beyond consideration, an ironic note from our present day perspective in reviewing the subsequent history of the Holocaust, a latter-day Inquisition. Notes Edwin B. Bronner in *Philadelphia: A 300 Year History*, "in the spirit of the Holy Experiment, by which term William Penn had meant above all religious freedom, there were no laws in Pennsylvania against freedom of worship so long as the worshippers recognized the suzerainty of God;" thus the relatively easy acceptance of Jews as well as Catholics.

Philadelphia, that city of Brotherly Love, was a good place for Levy to have landed. By 1760 when he arrived, the city had achieved a level of sophistication. Many church spires thrust skyward, streets were paved, and the State House tower housed its new Liberty Bell, as yet uncracked. Since its founding in 1682 by William Penn with Quaker artisans and merchants, Philadelphia now had 20,000 inhabitants. A library, a college, a hospital, bookshops and many coffee houses, social clubs and taverns enriched the lives of the inhabitants. The arts in the form of painting, theater, dance and music flourished. Cabinetmakers, silversmiths and goldsmiths, clock and watchmakers and crafters of fine instruments found ready markets among the prosperous Philadelphians.

Ben Franklin, back home after a long European stay, had redesigned the whale-oil street lamps, organized the postal system and published *The Pennsylvania Gazette* and *Poor Richard's Almanac.* At least partially due to Franklin's experiments in electricity, Philadelphia came to be considered the center of a flowering American civilization. The great Philadelphia Wagon Road to Lancaster opened a southerly route for settlers heading west and traders returning east. It was to be expanded into what was later known as the Lincoln Highway or Route 30, which eventually crossed to Pittsburgh in the southwest corner of the state, and beyond to Ohio. The northern route, where Routes 45 and 80 exist today, was still a wilderness, yet to be developed.

Like so many other immigrants, Levy chose to come to this strange polyglot society in Philadelphia without knowledge of the English language. Within a brief time, he had connected with other Jewish families, principally the Gratzes, Simons and Ettings, and possibly some distant relatives. Barnard and Michael Gratz, who arrived a few years earlier from England, were just about his age. They opened the doors of commerce and Indian trade to their new friend.

It was a "town of entrepreneurs," according to Sam Bass Warner, Jr. in *The Private City.* "Philadelphia had settlers, natural resources, capital, religious freedom and comparatively little government." Colonial trade was booming, exporting furs, lumber, barrel staves, pig and bar iron, wheat and flour; importing linens from Ireland, wine from Madeira and Portugal, English woolens and cutlery, and rum, molasses and "parcels" of slaves (to the chagrin of Quaker merchants) from the West Indies. It was an ideal setting for a budding entrepreneur.

Before long, through his new friends, Levy had established a healthy business as an Indian trader. In addition, he and the Gratzes speculated extensively in the purchase of tracts of undeveloped land, a privilege unknown to European Jews who in most European countries were traditionally denied the right to own property.

I marvel at the challenges of a new culture faced by Aaron Levy, even the new skills of wilderness survival to a city boy, superimposed on strict adherence to his orthodox Jewish roots and traditions. Picture his first meeting with Native Americans. Philip Fithian, a young Presbyterian minister who kept a journal during a preaching tour of the Virginia-Pennsylvania frontier in 1775-1776 describes the natives as having, "the outside Rim of their Ears slitted and it hangs dangling strangely—Some have Rings, & others Drops of Silver in their Noses & Ears—ruffled Shirts, but many of these are very greasy—On the Trees near their Camps are painted with Red & Black Colours many wild and ferocious Animals—in the most furious gestures." Sightings of similar slits, mutilations and tattoos are, if not frequent, certainly visible on Philadelphia's streets today. But Fithian would probably be shocked to see that now they adorn the ears, noses and various body parts of teenagers in faded blue jeans, bare-midriffed tee shirts, and assorted flamboyant-colored hair.

Levy most likely spent his first ten years settling into his new country, first Philadelphia and then Lancaster, during which time he married Rachel Phillips, whose Ashkenazi roots were the same as his own. An apocryphal story has their original chance meeting in Philadelphia one Saturday, when Aaron came upon a weeping Rachel scrubbing the front steps of the Chew family house on Third Street. Benjamin Chew was a prominent lawyer who numbered the Penn family among his clients. Rachel was their indentured servant. But this was her Sabbath, a day supposedly guaranteed to be free from labor, a fact that her masters were not honoring. Apparently, soon afterward, Aaron Levy paid for her release from servitude, but probably not from housework, for they were married within weeks. By 1774, the couple was already settled and well established in the new village of Northumberland.

Northumberland was strategically located as a trading post at a point where the two branches of the Susquehanna River diverge, deep in Indian Territory, and about 150 miles northwest of Philadelphia, an arduous journey of about five days. In 1775, Philip Fithian describes in his *Journal* the boomtown frontier atmosphere with the village overflowing with boatmen, as "busy and noisy as a Philadelphia ferry-house." According to Dr. Fish's biography of Levy, "Aaron Levy's business during this period consisted mainly in supplying provisions, equipment and other needs to the local and neighboring farmers and in purchasing their produce, as well as in Indian trading, and in furnishing supplies to the military units and government agents stationed in that area." He also did his patriotic duty by serving in the Northumberland state militia.

Three years earlier there are records of Levy's purchase of land in Sunbury, a sister village across the Susquehanna from Northumberland, formerly the home of Shikellamy, a distinguished Cayuga chief. But Northumberland was where Aaron chose to build a home on land he bought from Reuben Haines, who, along with General James Potter, a hero who fought alongside General George Washington, had acquired most of the land that today is Centre County. It was Haines who cut the road from Northumberland through the Narrows to Spring Mills, part of which is today's Route 45.

Levy was well positioned in Northumberland to learn of profitable land deals in this expansive frontier environment. Following in the footsteps of Potter and Haines, and having gained assurance from his experience as a trader and provisioner, he developed a mastery of diving into the wilderness to carve out his own territory. Dr. Fish lists no records of land purchase, but starting in 1778, deed records show the sale by Rachel and Aaron Levy of town lots in Northumberland and large acreage on Loyalsock Creek, on the east branch of the Susquehanna River.

Among the more than 100 recorded deeds are some listed with acreage which he named: "Aaron's Fancy," 152 acres in Mahoning Township; "Aronton" and "Aronmore," 116 acres each in Bloom Township; "Aaron's Staff," in Buffalo Township; "Levy's Delight," in Lycoming County; "Levy's Grove," in Northumberland County; and "Levyburg," 371 acres in Bald Eagle Township. He obviously relished immortalizing his name on the map. Hundreds of thousands of acres passed through his hands. But the only bloc to which he gave his full attention, as well as his name, in terms of planning, designing, selling and supporting afterwards as a community, was the 334 acres he named "Aaronsburg," then in Northumberland County, which, in 1800, was to become part of the newly designated Centre County.

May 23, 1786

To the Public:

The subscriber begs to inform the public that he hath laid out a town called Aaronsburg, in the county of Northumberland, very pleasantly situated, in that beautiful, healthy and fertile settlement called Penns Valley. Plans of the town to be seen, and tickets to be had

*at Philadelphia, at Pottstown, at Reading, at Lancaster, at Carlisle,
at Yorktown, and of the subscriber at the town of Northumberland,
aforesaid.*

(Signed) Aaron Levy

What made Aaronsburg unique to Levy? Probably its location, in
what was then considered the geographic center of the state. It was situated on a road leading to Philadelphia, with a new road to Pittsburgh
expected to link up with it. And this valley promised fertile farmland,
timber and quarries, worked by the 20 odd families already settled there.
In the broadside for a lottery to sell town lots, Levy states that the town's
location "recommends itself as one of the first situations on the continent for an inland town." Pittsburgh might have disagreed with this
particular sales hype!

In general, Levy used Sunbury and Northumberland as models for
his new town. But from the way he laid out the town plan in 1786,
with Aaron's Square its 150-foot-wide main street heading northeast to
southwest, following the natural contours of the valley, he had visions
of Aaronsburg as the potential new capital of Pennsylvania. Aaron's
Square was "to remain free, clear, and unobstructed for public uses."
Levy intended its open grassy space "to facilitate publick discourse on
governmental matters." He put aside and planned to donate land for
schools and churches and burying grounds of all denominations. The

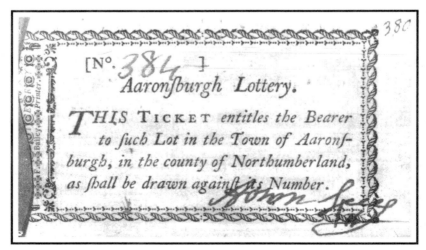

Aaronsburg Lottery Ticket. Courtesy Penns Valley Historical Association.

main east-west cross street he named Rachel's Way after his wife. He added a water system and streetlights, unusual amenities for that time.

The lottery Levy organized for the sale of land was obviously successful. The plan was to sell numbered tickets at six dollars each for lots ranging in size from 55 by 190 to 60 by 230 feet. A public drawing would take place after 300 lots were sold. There would be an additional charge of one-dollar yearly ground rent, or alternately full and clear title, for "20 Spanish silver milled dollars." In 1799, the town boasted 32 families and a post office. By 1802, most of the prime lots along Aaron Square were taken. Houses were set back behind the grassy space, giving an open and welcoming air. A census for the year shows three stores, a tavern keeper, a joiner, a gunsmith, a blacksmith, a wagon maker, a tanner, a hatter, a shoemaker, and a physician. Aaronsburg became the town in which to rest and refurbish before resuming the long trek west.

But Levy didn't rest. There were still more lots and adjacent farmland to sell, as well as delinquent purchasers to pursue. As promised, he turned over land for the newly organized churches, burying grounds and schools, and even recommended a preacher for the Lutheran congregation. His proprietary interest and good will extended to his gift of the pewter communion set that Bruce told me about. Curiously, nowhere is it indicated that he ever gave serious thought to settling there himself.

Earlier, during the Great Runaway, the Levys, like many of their neighbors, retreated from the frontier town of Northumberland to the safety of the town of Lancaster, about 90 miles to the south and 65 miles west of Philadelphia. They escaped British-encouraged Indian raids, during which settlers in Penns Valley were slaughtered and scalped, and their homes burned. H. C. Bell, in his *History of Northumberland*, quotes an eyewitness account of William Maclay who, along with Robert Morris, were the first United States Senators from Pennsylvania:

> "I left Sunbury and almost all my whole property on Wednesday last . . . I never in my life saw such a scene of distress. The river and the roads leading down to it were covered with men, women and children, flying for their lives, many without any property at all, and none who had not left the greatest part behind; in short Northumberland County is broken up."

During his five years in Lancaster, Levy became a partner in trade of Joseph Simon, the first Jew to settle there, and also the last Jewish survivor there at his death in 1804. Levy also deepened his relationship with his friends, the Gratzes. Childless and desiring an heir, Aaron and Rachel virtually adopted the oldest of Michael Gratz's sons, Simon, giving him full power of attorney. The Gratzes had extensive dealings for over 20 years with Robert Morris, who was also a financier, land speculator, and prominent signer of the Declaration of Independence. Levy became an associate of Morris and through him loaned money, some of it never repaid, to the Continental Congress during the Revolutionary War. Morris had his hand in many real estate deals at the time, and Levy worked with him as surveyor and investor, particularly in dealing with vast unsettled northern tracts.

After his return to Northumberland in 1783, land speculation was Levy's prime interest. He bought and sold land grants, and acted as purchasing agent for Morris, trekking for weeks into the wilderness himself to discover and claim virgin tracts in yet unspoken-for territory. An agreement between Levy, Morris and a Walter Stewart, in 1792, states, in part:

> *"That the said Aaron Levy will find out and discover a Tract or Tracts of Land the full quantity of at least forty thousand Acres not already taken up on the north side of the large West branch of the Susquehanna River & West side of little Mushanan Creek running into said River . . . And that for the discovery of the said Lands and the time and trouble of the said Aaron Levy . . . the said Aaron Levy shall have and receive from the said Robert Morris and Walter Stewart the Sum of fifteen Pounds Pennsylvania Currency per thousand Acres . . .*
> *"*

Morris and Stewart would pay for all Warrants and Surveys and the "reasonable Cost and Expenses of Chaincarriers Pack Horses and Provisions."

One of Levy's competitors, Samuel Wallis, with whom Levy was frequently in litigation, received a note from his agent, McClure, in the spring of 1793. It was found among Wallis' papers, written at their camp near Little Mushanan Creek:

> *"Samuel Wallis, Esq.: 'Dear Sir, I send the bearer to hurry up the warrants. Levy and his party have gone up the Susquehanna from the Great Island (Williamsport) in a canoe; and as these lands are rich in quality, hurry on the warrants."*

Between April and June of 1794, Levy contracted for, and delivered to James Wilson, almost 500,000 acres in Northumberland, Mifflin and

Huntingdon Counties. He was to be paid in specie (gold or silver money current in Pennsylvania at the time) in three equal installments in 1795, 1796 and 1797.

When the land boom collapsed, Levy had land but no cash. In the December 1796 entry in his *Commonplace Book*, Benjamin Rush comments: "This month great distress pervaded our city from failures, &c. 150, it is said, occurred in 6 weeks, and 67 people went to jail," including Robert Morris and his partner John Nicholson. By 1802, Levy had turned over most of his interests in the Aaronsburg and other properties to Simon Gratz for "one Eagle."

He and Rachel were getting on in years. No co-religionists settled permanently in Northumberland, and keenly feeling their isolation, despite having made many good friends including the future Governor Simon Snyder, they decided to move back to Philadelphia. There Jews, according to Wolf and Whiteman in *The History of the Jews of Philadelphia from Colonial Times to the Age of Jackson*, had "high visibility" and were an integral part of the community. The designation "gentleman" was attached to his name, where earlier tax records in Sunbury had him listed as first "shopkeeper," later upgraded to "merchant."

In Philadelphia Levy was a member and financial contributor to the library founded by Benjamin Franklin. He helped found Mikveh Israel, one of the nation's first synagogues. Thus, happily relocated in their house on Mulberry Street, with all the appurtenances of wealth, books, silver and miniature paintings, in the company of old friends, in an urban environment, similar to that from whence they came originally, but with the security of a William Penn designed social and religious society, the aging husband and wife spent the rest of their days in comfort. In his will, Aaron Levy left to Simon Gratz's sister, Rebecca, "my gilt silver oval Sugar Bowl with lid and Silver Bowl with lid." Rebecca, incidentally, was the inspiration for Walter Scott's Rebecca in *Ivanhoe*.

How do we evaluate the life of Aaron Levy? Or, more interestingly, how would he have evaluated his life? I think he would have been more than pleased. By daring to come to the New World, he found opportunities and privileges he never could have had, or even dreamed of having, in the Old World. He flourished in the freedom made possible by the fair climate of religious tolerance in Pennsylvania, as envisioned in William Penn's dream of a Holy Experiment.

Actually, it was not quite Penn's dream. To Penn, as a Quaker, his concept of religious freedom included all Protestant sects, and went so far as to include the despised Catholics, or Papists, Christians all. Jews didn't even enter into Penn's consciousness in England, nor in his planning of his new colony. But the wording of his charter was broad and did not discriminate.

Aaron Levy took full advantage of these opportunities. He was obviously an adaptable pragmatist, successful in business as a merchant and land speculator in his adopted country: an entrepreneur, a venturer into uncharted territory, who opened up the way of westward expansion for others. Unlike his neighbor, Joseph Priestley, and earlier, William Penn, who dealt principally in ideas and who saw land as a symbol of wealth and status, a chance to become landed gentry, Levy's attitude towards land was as a commodity, to buy and trade and sell. In other words, a new American spirit, a new American capitalist!

In terms of a heritage in his adopted land, Levy did not fulfill his dream of having his name live on attached to the capital of the state of Pennsylvania. Aaronsburg never became the capital of the state, or even the county seat of Centre County. Those were distinctions given to Harrisburg and Bellefonte. Aaronsburg remains the same small village with a population today no bigger than when he developed it over 200 years ago. But Levy succeeded in a manner that he could never have imagined, and which would have left him speechless. Through the vagaries of fate, a relatively small gesture of consideration to the elders of the Christian churches of Aaronsburg by this minority entrepreneur catapulted the name of Aaron Levy into Pennsylvania history, albeit 150 years after his death.

Aaronsburg town sign. Photo by Joan Morse Gordon.

Chapter 5

IDEALISTS & REALISTS

The New World in general and Pennsylvania in particular captivated many intellectuals in the Old World. Some of them actually emigrated; others did not but were inspired throughout their lives and careers by the idea of the new land. My fascination with the people and past along Route 45 soon extended to a need to explore this broader realm.

Joseph Priestley

On Bastille Day, July 14, 1791, the second anniversary of the onset of the French Revolution, Joseph Priestley was forced to flee his home and pulpit in Birmingham, England, one step ahead of an aroused mob. As a prominent member of the Constitutional Society of Birmingham, he was expected to attend a public dinner at a local hotel on the night of July 14th to celebrate the fall of the Bastille. Well-meaning friends constrained him from participating, since Priestley was an outspoken Nonconformist and Unitarian minister, in opposition to the established Anglican Church, and therefore, an obvious target for attack.

When government sponsored rioters burst in on the diners and discovered Priestley wasn't in attendance, they went on a rampage, goaded by agitators, pillaging and burning his and other members' homes and churches. Shouting "King and Church" as they swarmed, the mob

Image of Joseph Priestley. Courtesy Special Collections Library, Pennsylvania State University.

burned Priestley's New Meetinghouse on High Street. They then went a mile and a half on to his home where, having no fire source, they destroyed his library and records of experiments by hand.

His crime? Priestley, like William Penn 100 years before him, was not a member of the dominant Church of England. Non-members, called Dissenters, were persecuted in many ways. They were refused admission to the major universities, specifically Oxford and Cambridge, and were also denied certain religious and civil posts. Priestley was targeted as a threat to the English monarchy. He had been an outspoken admirer of the revolution in France when it was an attempt to reform the current government following the English model of a constitutional monarchy. Later, when the revolution turned into a Reign of Terror, he condemned it, a point lost on the English monarchy.

While under this tremendous pressure, Priestley, already in his sixties, slowly and reluctantly agreed to cut his tenuous ties and join his three sons who, with his support, had left the year earlier and were attempting to establish a community in the New World for liberal dissenters. Priestley's friend, Brissot de Warville, a French humanitarian, in his *New Travels in the United States of America*, published in England in 1792, wrote of his dream of such an undertaking. As early as 1768, Priestley expressed his longing for an open-minded environment, in his *Essay on the First Principles of Government*, declaring:

> *"Let all the friends of liberty and human nature join to free the minds of men from the shackles of narrow and impolitic laws. Let us be free ourselves, and leave the blessings of freedom to our posterity."*

Priestley was a polymath. Besides his major contribution to science in the discovery of oxygen, he wrote and lectured extensively on philosophy, metaphysics, divinity, history and politics. Joseph Johnson,

Dr. Priestley's House and Laboratory, Fair Hill. Destroyed in the Birmingham Riots, 14 July 1791. From the Priestley Memorial Scrapbook, 1875. *Courtesy Special Collections Library, Pennsylvania State University.*

who dared to publish Priestley's inflammatory prose, made it a habit of entertaining friends at Sunday dinner. Among the regular guests in this "radical circle" were Priestley, Erasmus Darwin, Thomas Paine, Samuel Taylor Coleridge, Benjamin Franklin, Henry Fuseli, Sir Josiah Wedgwood, Mary Wollstonecraft and William Blake. In 1784, Blake wrote a satire, *An Island in the Moon*, in which Priestley, much to his amusement, is parodied as Mr. Inflammable Gass. This is just a glimpse of the stimulating world of the intellect Priestley reluctantly left behind in England, "being at a time of life in which I could not expect much satisfaction as to friends and society, comparable to that which I left."

Upon their arrival in America in 1794, Priestley and his wife, Mary, were warmly welcomed first in New York, by Governor DeWitt Clinton among others; and then in Philadelphia, where, Benjamin Rush states, "I waited on him, and spent about half an hour in his company. He related many instances of the persecuting conduct of the church and court towards him." Rush was a Philadelphia-born, European-trained physician, a signer of the Declaration of Independence in 1776, and the Constitution in 1787, founder of the first anti-slavery society in America, and Professor of Medicine at the University of Pennsylvania; certainly the perfect person to head Priestley's welcoming committee.

At dinner, on an evening shortly afterward, discussing his Unitarian beliefs, Priestley revealed to Rush that Benjamin Franklin, a good friend of his in England, was a Deist like himself. Rush became a good friend and physician of Priestley, and attended him through his last illness. While in Philadelphia, Rush offered him a professorship in Chemistry at the University of Pennsylvania. But Priestley and his wife chose to settle in the small town of Northumberland on the Susquehanna River, to be nearer their sons and their planned community of Friends of Liberty.

Seventeen ninety-four was the same year Aaron Levy, age 52 and tiring of frontier life, moved from his Northumberland home to Philadelphia. Although Northumberland contained only "160 dwellings," we have no specific knowledge of any encounter between the neighbors during the year in which their stay overlapped. Since the town was so small I find it hard to believe that their paths never crossed. Levy was a staunch Federalist, while Priestley was a Jeffersonian; Levy, a Jew, and Priestley, a Unitarian. However, in all probability, the community that Priestley's sons planned to establish to the north along the Loyalsock Creek was on 700,000 acres of land in whose sale and survey Levy had a hand while working for Robert Morris. Priestley's sons and a friend, Thomas Cooper, through Robert Morris, bought the large tract of land with the idea of establishing a haven, the Friends of Liberty, for English religious and political dissidents, a community over which the elder Priestley would presumably preside.

Meanwhile, back in England in 1794, Cooper distributed *Some Information Respecting America*, a pamphlet he wrote in the form of letters to an interested friend, glorifying life in the newly independent country. Like William Penn, 100 years earlier, this was Cooper's means of advertising and selling the land in which he and the young Priestleys had invested.

Presupposing that his friend has modest means, Cooper advises him to go "where land is cheap and fertile . . . and if poſſible in the neighbourhood of a few Engliſh, whoſe ſociety, even in America, is intereſting to an Engliſh ſettler." Carefully and subtly he narrows the reader's interest to his own property on the Susquehanna in Pennsylvania. He compares and contrasts the climate and quality of other land available, pointing out the danger from hostile Indians, and subtly questioning the class of settlers in the South and New England. Of New Jersey he maligns, "Mufquitoes and agues are more troublefome . . . " Of upstate New York he disparages, "the rivers are fluggish, the country flat . . . and not a mountain to be found from the Genefee river to the falls of Niagara." He hints . . . "the peach, I believe, does not perfectly ripen at Albany." He dismisses Kentucky and Maryland as "hot and moist." On a more serious note these states used slave labor to which Cooper was unalterably opposed. And, as a clincher "the road in going and returning, both by Pittfburg and the Wildernef is liable to perpetual molestation by the savages."

In October of 1794, only four months after their own arrival, the Priestleys were visited by William Davy, an Englishman, also recently arrived, who records in his diary a trip he took to look at lands in the north with the prospect of convincing some English families to settle. His comments are more practical than poetic:

> *"Friday Septr 26th at 4 o'Clock P.M. I left German Town in a one Horse Chair accompanied by Mr. Joseph Priestley Junr. & Mr. Madge on Mr. Priestley's Horse & proceeded over Chestnut Hill to Norristown, the Roads very rough & in consequence of heavy rains having fallen yesterday are washed & cut into deep Gulleys. Some part of the country we pass'd through is wild and uncultivated, the Hills are yet covered with Woods & in a state of Nature, but the Valleys are rich and fertile producing heavy Crops of Grass & Clover, & have improved Farms and Settlements on them."*

The people are well dressed, "even though the Cloathing is plain . . . There is a great simplicity in their Manners." "The Farmer & Waggoner eats his own Provisions & sleeps in his cover'd Waggon." [a Conestoga wagon made in the vicinity]. "Many travel a hundred Miles without spending sixpence on the Road & on Market Days & Nights the Streets are crowded with these economical Germans.

By September 30th, the travelers have crossed the summit of Blue Mountain,

> *"13 Miles of which we walk'd a great part over Rockey, Craggy Precipices, deep Swamps, rapid ascents, & in the best places very stony Roads & truly dangerous to a Carriage . . . Panthers, Bears, Pole Cats, Squirrels & Deer are the principal Inhabitants of these Regions."*

After five days journey they arrive in Sunbury on October first.

> *"Thursday Octr. 2d. Dr. Priestley visited us at Sunbury looks healthy*
> *& Cheerful. Has left off his Perriwig & Combs his short grey locks in*
> *the true style of the simplicity of the Country. He is on the whole so*
> *well pleased that he is preparing to build a very good Brick House the*
> *Foundation of which & a Well he has already dug."*

Davy and Priestley, Jr. continue their trip north with the land speculator Samuel Wallis, Aaron Levy's rival, and stay as his guest at Muncy
Farm, an imposing stone "mansion," situated in the West Branch Valley
on land extending six miles on both sides of the Susquehanna. Back
once again in Northumberland, Davy checks out available nearby property, still without making a commitment. Eventually, he and Priestley,
Jr. buy a small 204 acre estate, permitting the former owner to stay on as
a tenant. On Monday the 13th Davy comments:

> *"Dr. Priestley appears perfectly pleased with his Situation & having a*
> *Printing Press close by him is a great Satisfaction & Entertainment, &*
> *he is now printing a Sequel to his Letters to French Philosophers & an*
> *answer to Pain's [Thomas Paine] Age of Reason (a Book much read*
> *in this Country). He is very anxious for the arrival here of his Books*
> *& Apparatus . . . that he may resume his favorite Studies, but still*
> *more anxious to get Society that he may again pursue his principal*
> *Object, by Publick Instruction in a Place of Worship, & by Lectures*
> *to Youth . . . The Doctor enjoys a game of Whist & altho he never*
> *hazards a farthing is highly diverted with playing good Cards but*
> *never ruffl'd by bad ones."*

The "Society" Priestley so eagerly desired was definitely not to be
found in the vicinity. Says Davy:

> *"I observe in the Inhabitants of this Country a great Apathy not*
> *attracted by any thing Novel in Art, or beautiful in Nature; the most*
> *respectable (even lawyers) have few or no Books, fine Cloaths, good*
> *Furniture, handsome Equipages."*

In conclusion, Davy decides:

> *" . . . that for People accustomed to Society it will by no means do*
> *to begin new Settlements. This must be done by Persons enured to*
> *Fatigue & hard Labour & content with any humble Fare & Seclusion,*
> *that on the contrary it will be a very happy and proffitable Situation*
> *to carry on Improvements on Estates of which enough is already*

clear'd for a Family to live on the Produce of, but it can only be made comfortable where a few Families unite in a neighborhood so as to assist in supplying each others Wants."

Davy followed his own advice, winding up as a successful merchant in Philadelphia, leaving the wilderness to others. The young Priestleys and Thomas Cooper eventually abandoned their land scheme due to their inability to attract sufficient buyers.

Joseph Priestley wrote to a friend of life in Northumberland:

"This place is inconveniently situated for carrying on my experiments; but living here is cheap, and the climate, &c., uncommonly fine, and my sons are settling in farms about me . . . But our great advantage arises from a happy constitution of government, and a state of peace, in consequence of which the country enjoys an unexampled state of prosperity, the advancement of population, and improvements of all kinds."

But even in this remote outpost, peace was hard to find. For someone who had expressed himself freely and courageously for so long in England, Priestley made his political views apparent in his new home, thus earning the enmity of the Federalist President John Adams who called Priestley "as weak as water." Priestley opposed Federalist ideas and came out against the Alien and Sedition Acts, requiring 14 years' residence in order to become a citizen, which could have impacted on him had he applied for citizenship. Priestley was called "an apostle of sedition," "a political viper," "a Jesuit!" Maligned to that extent, he wrote as a reply *Letters to the Inhabitants of Northumberland and its Neighbourhood* in 1797, explaining his views on the French Revolution, the American Constitution, and religion:

"I think it barely possible for a man who has, in the five years that I have been among you, done so little of an offensive nature, to have become the object of more suspicion and rancour than I have incurred."

Another disappointment for Priestley was the lack of interest he found for his Unitarian faith in Northumberland. As there were never enough members to support a congregation, he regularly led a few fellow English exiles in services in his or his son's home. It wasn't until 1834, long after his grandfather's death, that Joseph Rayner Priestley built a small chapel which survives today as the Joseph Priestley Memorial and houses a Unitarian Universalist congregation.

Poets Southey & Coleridge Dream of a New World Utopia

Seventeen ninety-four, the year the Priestleys arrived in America, was a trying time for two young English university students hemmed in by political and personal despair. Earlier, they were caught up by the exciting possibilities of Liberty, Equality and Fraternity proclaimed by the French Revolution; now, they were horrified by its perversion into the Reign of Terror which was responsible for the death by guillotine of some of their French revolutionary idols.

Robert Southey, 19, a student at Oxford, and Samuel Taylor Coleridge, 22, at Cambridge, were on a parallel track of difficulties both academic and economic. Their careers had no direction. Both were dependent on family who pressured the young men in return for financial assistance to choose paths other than poetry, a muse they shared.

Coleridge, the youngest of a family of ten, and the only boy, was sent off to school at Christ's Hospital when he was eight, after his father's death. Later on at Cambridge, he won scholastic awards but was always in debt. To escape his debtors he enlisted in the Light Dragoons using the *nom de guerre* Silas Tomkyn Comberbacke. Silas was a rotten soldier, always falling off his horse and losing his rifle. Friends eventually retrieved him and brought him back to Cambridge. He left, nevertheless, without a degree. It was then, by chance, Coleridge's path crossed Southey's when he stopped by to visit a friend at Oxford while on a walking tour of Wales. Recognizing their common dilemma, the friend arranged a meeting. The two found much in common: poetry, deism, discontent with society, dreams of democracy, and lack of any better prospects. Together they moved to Bristol to work on the idea of starting a commune in the New World, America, which would be based on mutual love and mutual ownership.

Coleridge, it turns out, was well steeped in information about the New World. He had read, and was stimulated creatively, by John Bartram's *Travels* (1791), an idyllic and poetic picture of American nature, written while collecting seeds and plants throughout the South; Crevecoeur's *Letters from an American Farmer* (1782), a paean to primitive America as an egalitarian paradise; and Thomas Cooper's *Some Information Respecting America*. Coleridge, a fellow Unitarian, loved and respected Dr. Priestley. The thought of bringing his and Southey's Pantisocracy, a perfect society of equals, to join the Priestley utopian experiment of perfectibility on the Susquehanna, (Susquehanna! Coleridge loved the sound of that word), spurred him on to find a practical way to make this dream a reality. To a friend, Southey wrote, "This new scheme has given me new life, new hope, new energy; all the faculties of my mind are dilated."

Five weeks later, with the outlines of a plan to cogitate on, Coleridge continued his walking tour, leaving behind with Southey a shared dream of an ideal republic in an ideal setting. As Southey wrote to his brother: "We preached Pantisocracy and Aspheterism everywhere. These, Tom, are two new words, the first signifying the equal government of all; and the other, the generalization of individual property."

The two friends' plan for their ideal community on the banks of the Susquehanna would start with the emigration the following spring of 12 young married couples "of good education and liberal principles," naturally themselves and friend Robert Lovell included, since each of the three men was attached to one of three sisters of the Fricker family. The Fricker family seems to have been best known for producing daughters sought after by struggling poets. The couples would spend concentrated time together beforehand to get to know each other well, clearly define their goals and expectations, and work out every ideological wrinkle. To a friend, Southey wrote:

> *"In the course of the winter those of us whose bodies, from habits of sedentary study or academic indolence, have not acquired our full time and strength, intend to learn the theory and practice of agriculture and carpentry, according as situation and circumstance make one or the other convenient."*

Once settled in their Pantisocracy, the poets figured, according to their reading of Adam Smith, that it would be sufficient that each man should labor two or three hours a day, working for the whole colony. A good library was essential, and their "leisure hours to be spent in study, liberal discussions, and the education of their children," as reported by a mutual friend and supporter, Thomas Poole. The role of women was relegated to the care of children and occupations compatible with their strength. "At the same time the greatest attention is to be paid to the cultivation of their minds." No limits were placed on political or religious freedom, except whatever might impact on the colony at large.

Coleridge and Southey calculated that 125 pounds would be sufficient to cover the initial expenses of each couple, and they set about finding the wherewithal. How do poets raise money? By writing, singly and together. The three, Coleridge, Southey and Lovell, would collaborate on a poetic drama, *The Fall of Robespierre*, each to write one act in

24 hours. But, not unexpectedly, Coleridge was late, Lovell didn't conform, and Southey had to rewrite. Individually, Southey's *Joan of Arc* and Coleridge's *Latin Poems*, were eventually published, but not in time for their current needs. They then tried lecturing: Coleridge, on politics and morals; Southey, on history.

As economic problems remained unresolved, other obstacles appeared. Southey wanted his aunt's manservant to be part of the group, as a servant. Coleridge's rejoinder was, "this is not our plan, nor can I defend it." Complete equality was essential to the success of their Pantisocracy.

Familial objections mounted, obstacles to the plan loomed larger, and finally overwhelmed them. After two years of actual labor, the Pantosocratic dream died aborning. But evidence of their reading and study and enthusiasm for the aborted adventure on the Susquehanna continued to enrich both Coleridge and Southey's poetic imagery for years to come.

The Asylum Company

In 1793, a year before Coleridge and Southey conceived of their Utopia-on-the-Susquehanna, two groups of French citizens, Loyalists escaping from the Reign of Terror in France and settlers escaping from a slave and mulatto uprising led by Toussaint-Louverture in Santo Domingo, (or Haiti) found themselves unceremoniously debarked in the crowded port of Philadelphia. Although they were given warm and temporary hospitality, some long-term solution for a permanent home had to be found. Here, the ubiquitous Robert Morris conveniently appeared and convinced them to buy some of his millions of acres of land holdings in northern Pennsylvania, not far from the New York border, as the site of a French community-in-exile, quite far from the hub and hubbub of New World civilization. This haven, subsequently named Azilum, or Asylum, was located on a wide horseshoe bend in the river known as Susquehanna, coincidentally not far from the Pantosocratic dream of Southey and Coleridge on the might-have-been Priestley lands. What a concentration of aristocracy and intellectualism that would have been!

These new arrivals from France came in desperation, seeking a haven from almost certain death and confiscation of their properties back home. They were all supporters of King Louis XVI, moderates who, while working with him towards more egalitarian rights for all Frenchmen, were overwhelmed by the Reign of Terror and forced to flee France for their lives. Courtiers, nobles, men of the cloth, merchants, army officers, plantation owners, theirs was neither a pioneering venture nor a search for a Utopia. Unlike the Loyalists whose hands had never been sullied, the escapees from Santo Domingo sugar plantations arrived with some slaves and some knowledge of farming.

Robert Morris and his partner in many land schemes, John Nicholson, who at that time were Pennsylvania's senator and comptroller general respectively, set up The Asylum Company along with two distinguished Frenchmen. Antoine Omer Talon, a lawyer who had been an advisor to the King, and Viscount Louis de Noailles, brother-in-law of Lafayette, who had fought with Washington against the British in our War of Independence, supervised the land deal and spearheaded the project. The plan called for the purchase of one million acres of the Morris/Nicholson land west of the north branch of the Susquehanna to the Loyalhanna, that they would divide into 5000 shares of 200 acres. This land, costing the Company 15 cents an acre was to be sold for a profitable three dollars per acre.

The first settlement was sited at a dramatic four-mile-wide horseshoe curve of the river called Standing Stone; a fertile plain backed by a

Share of Asylum Company. Courtesy French Azilum, Inc.

grand sweep of mountains. Their town plan, unlike Aaron Levy's plan for Aaronsburg, was a square grid pattern of half-acre lots with wide streets and a two-acre market place in its center, similar to many towns in France. Surrounding the town were larger lots for industry and farming. Within the first year 30 log houses were built. They were rough, but still included refinements such as glass windows with shutters, porches and wallpaper. A piano was reported having been seen in one of the log houses by a visitor in 1798. The settlers, unaccustomed to manual labor, hired workers for the actual building. Nevertheless, they were busy planting gardens and orchards, raising cattle and organizing essential small industries. Market Square soon was rimmed with shops, practical and fashionable, a chapel, a school, and a theater. A theater and the latest Paris fashions bloomed in the wilderness. I can't help but muse on the difference in priorities of these displaced Parisians and the Palatines who settled in Aaronsburg. A theater? Fashions?

Close to the river, they built an impressive three-story log building, 84 feet long and 60 feet wide, with "massive" doors and fireplaces. It was used for concerts, card parties, formal dances and other public gatherings. Dancers wore satin gowns and knee breeches and buckled dancing slippers. By tradition it was called the Queen's House. Legend has it that this Grande Maison was intended to be the new home of Marie Antoinette and her son, the Dauphin, when they were to be smuggled out of prison and whisked away prior to an encounter with the guillotine. Tragically for the Queen, the rescuers were too late.

The community thrived for a few years despite many colonists' difficulty in acclimating to their new environment. Distinguished visitors who graced the community included the surviving Dauphin and future king, Louis Philippe, Tallyrand and the Duc de la Rochefoucauld-Liancourt who, during a 12-day visit to Azilum in 1795 gives fascinating insights in his journal:

> "One of the greateſt impediments to the proſperity of this ſettlement will probably ariſe from the prejudices of ſome Frenchmen againſt the Americans, unleſs ſelf-intereſt and reaſon ſhould prove the means of removing them—ſome of them vauntingly declare, that they will never learn the language of the country, or enter into converſation with an American."

Although he admits "a more convenient ſpot might, doubtless, have been chosen," he sees the necessity for "inviting induſtrious ſettlers" and "endeavoring to meliorate the breedſ of horſes and cattle," he gently chides:

" . . . however polifhed its prefent inhabitants may be, the gentleman cannot eafily difpenfe with the affiftance of the artift and the hufbandman, as thefe can without the gentleman."

The Asylum Company had trouble from the start. They were under financed and unable to lure a sufficient number of settlers to this Paris-on-the Susquehanna. Land titles were under dispute. Early on Morris and Nicholson withdrew into bankruptcy to the tune of one million dollars, leaving the burden of the struggling settlement to Talon and de Noailles. And, wasn't it likely that their million acres here, stretching from the Susquehanna to the Loyalsock, and the 700,000 acres proposed for the Priestley utopia on the Loyalsock might have overlapped at least a little?

The colony limped along. Some settlers gradually moved to warmer climes, some back to Santo Domingo. When, in 1803, Napoleon assured others that they were now welcome back to France with their properties restored, their lives no longer in jeopardy, exile was over. The abandoned refuge was eventually plowed under and planted in grain by a local farmer.

Not everyone left the area. One still finds traces in French place and family names. Binghamton University students are excavating the glorious site in an archeological dig. Bits of window glass, nails and pottery fragments are carefully sifted. Foundations of houses and outbuildings are being uncovered.

La Grande Maison. Courtesy French Azilum, Inc.

Now leveled to a verdant plain, I observe from on high the graceful horseshoe curve from across the river and read the bronze historic marker:

AZILUM
The broad plain which can
be seen from this point
was the site, 1793-1803, of
the French refugee colony.
The Great House, built for
Marie Antoinette and her
son, was there and an
entire village founded.

————————

Chapter 6

SETTLER & UNSETTLER

When I first came to this area I heard much about the determined and tenacious people who settled here, particularly immigrants from the German Palatine. I found those stories to be true, but so are stories of individuals whose talents were put to other, more notorious uses.

From the Palatine to Permanent Settlement

When I would ask old timers in Penns Valley where their ancestors hailed from, I most often got a vague reply. "Somewhere in Germany," they'd say. But they were not sure where. The only thing that many of these fourth or fifth generation Penns Valley natives are certain is that it must have been a place just like "here." Many of the forebears of the current residents came from the Palatinate on the Rhine, an exceptionally fine area for agriculture due, as Peirce Lewis says, to its friable loess sub-soil, similar to the soil in Penns Valley. According to John Hostetler in *Amish Society*, the language known as Pennsylvania Dutch, still spoken today in the heavily settled German areas of Pennsylvania, is based on a Palatine dialect, a strong indication of its source. Many of the old-timers in Penns Valley either speak or understand Pennsylvania Dutch, thus enabling them to communicate with their Amish neighbors.

The Palatines took quite a circuitous route to arrive at the peace they eventually found in these valleys. Whereas William Penn, Aaron Levy, and Joseph Priestley left the Old World from their home ports and sailed directly to Philadelphia, the early settlers from the Palatinate came to central Pennsylvania by stages. Their journey was not only circuitous, but in many cases, tortuous.

The Rhine Valley in the Palatinate, a well-worn pathway to the heart of Germany for the invading French, was the battleground for foreign wars for more than 1,000 years. The principal causes of these wars were the desire for additional territory and religious differences, a battle between Catholics and Protestants. In succession, Charlemagne, the Saxons, and Papal Rome ran roughshod over the valley. The people, although in the thrall of their own princes and great landowners, rose up in 1520 after their land holdings had been subdivided, leaving plots too small to farm. The standard they held high as they marched for the short-lived revolt was a peasant's clog on a pole.

Spain invaded the Palatine in 1620 during the Thirty Years' War, with England coming to its defense. After 1648, agriculture was at a standstill, many villages were deserted, and the population was moving to cities. Their stock destroyed and their homes burned, the peasants were totally dependent on the nobles and landowners, since they had no capital or credit. In 1668, the war between France and Spain was renewed and much of Europe was pulled into the conflict that lasted ten years.

During the French invasion of 1708, King Louis XIV was still seeking to eradicate Protestants, and, at the same time, grab more land. In the process, his army of 50,000 burned, pillaged and slaughtered 30,000 Protestant Palatines, a long time before the common use of the phrase "ethnic cleansing." The winter of 1708 was the coldest in 100 years. The rivers were icebound and the seacoast frozen, and vineyards and fruit trees were killed, leaving the peasants with nothing salvageable.

According to the Treaty of Westphalia, their leaders, the Electors Palatine, like other princes of the Holy Roman Empire with titles like count, duke, king, and margrave, could force the peasants to submit to the Elector's faith. Over a period of 130 years, they switched back and forth from Reform to Lutheran. The current Elector broke the chain and adhered to the Church of Rome, pressuring his subjects to convert. This latest incursion on their religious beliefs was the final straw.

The inhabitants had little left to look forward to, but there was one way out. During these later oppressive years, they had been wooed by agents of the British Crown and William Penn, who traveled up and down the Rhine as early as 1677, extolling the benefits of a life in the

New World, promising them land of their own and the possibility of religious freedom in a non-sectarian Christian community. England's Queen Anne provided additional assistance. It was in England's self-interest to people their colonies with non-English, who could not then claim all of the rights and privileges of English citizens. And, in the process, the Queen was championing the Protestant cause in Europe.

In response to a Palatine petition to the British Board of Trade, the Crown and Parliament agreed to finance the Palatines' transportation to the colonies so that they would develop land in the Crown's vast unoccupied possessions in America. The cost was estimated at eight pounds per emigrant. Seven thousand started the first phase of a mass exodus of Palatines down the Rhine in a trip that lasted from four to six weeks. The Palatine Elector, who could have stopped the departure of the few, was powerless to halt such a large number of émigrés. The Protestant Consistory in the Palatinate was chagrined at the negative image to the point of issuing a denial of religious persecution. Along the Rhine River route sympathetic Protestant families formed a kind of underground railway, giving succor to the escapees.

By June, about 1,000 Palatines were arriving in Rotterdam every week. Those who continued on to London were placed outside the city walls in the equivalent of displaced persons' tent camps that offered minimum comfort. Earlier in the year, a Royal proclamation was finally issued in German, to the effect that any Palatine arriving after October would be sent back to Germany. By November, the numbers had reached over 30,000. The British government was totally unprepared for this onslaught and tried to move the Palatines out quickly and efficiently.

William Penn was in bad financial straits himself at this time in 1709, having just been released after serving nine months in debtors' prison, so he was unable to help the Palatines directly. Nevertheless, in supporting the exodus, he made clear "the interest of England to improve and thicken her colonys with people not her own." He was the author of a bill granting naturalization for foreign Protestants, as a result of a petition from a Pennsylvanian German. Walter Knittle, in *The Early Palatine Emigration*, states the law provided that those naturalized:

> " . . . *had to take an oath of allegiance; had to partake of the sacrament according to Anglican ritual before witnesses who signed a certificate to that effect; had the right to purchase and hold land which might be transmitted to one's children; and could take part in trade and commerce, usually forbidden to foreigners.*"

Boats from London were packed to more than capacity with minimal provisions, sanitary facilities and potable drinking water. Some of the Palatines were taken on a short voyage to settle in Ireland, thereby raising the Protestant population quota. However, the largest number made the long, arduous voyage to America. The eight pounds allocated for each passenger's transatlantic passage did not go far. At sea, unscrupulous ships' masters and crews took advantage of their passengers, who were treated like cargo. Many became ill and died during the voyage.

Before leaving England, they had signed contracts written in English, which practically none of the German-speaking peasants understood, for money to be paid by them on debarkation in return for their passage. When they arrived in Philadelphia, many were sold into a kind of indentured slavery, in order to raise the money to pay back their debt. The ones who could pay were free to go.

Another group landed in New York and was sent upstate to produce ships' stores for the British navy. The treacherous New York Governor Hunter duped them out of land they already had under cultivation. In disgust, and led by Conrad Weiser, diplomat and Indian negotiator, they eventually migrated south, down the Susquehanna to the Tulpehocken to seek asylum in the more liberal state of Pennsylvania. After a while the Palatines spread out into Berks and Lebanon Counties. By this time the second generation spread further west to our Penns Valley. For the Palatines who arrived in New York, the promise of owning and cultivating their own land took much longer than the refugees had anticipated.

By 1775, Germans represented about one-third of the population of Pennsylvania, the majority of them farmers. Their tradition of farming went back 30 generations in the old country, where they worked others' fields as tenant farmers. These were small plots from which the maximum return was demanded. Experience in intensive farming enabled the settlers, once they had cleared the land, to establish the same productive practices on their own farms. Settling in and extending their holdings to support their large families followed. Secure in their religion, which now they were free to practice, they were industrious, frugal and not afraid of *Arbeit*, or hard labor, which for them was the norm. These characteristics are still to be found today in their descendants tending their farms in Penns Valley.

Robber Lewis

Every region has its myths and legends, heroes and villains. David Lewis, also known as "Robber Lewis," more than fills the bill for Penns and Buffalo Valleys and beyond, providing a striking contrast with the original settlers. Though widely believed to be a Robin Hood who took from the rich and gave to the poor, the records show he took more than he gave away, more in the tradition of a latter-day Sundance Kid than the hero of Sherwood Forest.

John Brinckerhoff Jackson says,

> *"So the true function of the road is to serve us by taking us home. Without a specific destination, a road has no reason for existing. Left to its own devices it tends to wander into the wider environment and disappear. It has another tendency, much more dangerous: to introduce unwanted outsiders into the self-sufficient community or house."*

This is where Lewis fits into our story. His role is a counterpoint to others I describe who found a road and a way of life and settled down permanently in central Pennsylvania. Although he was a native to the area, David Lewis became the unwanted rootless outsider. He wandered ceaselessly using the road only as a conduit for his criminal escapades; its byways were his vantage point for ambush and holdup.

The youngest of ten children, Lewis was said to have been born in either Carlisle or Bellefonte, Pennsylvania in March of 1788 or 1790, the son of Lewis Lewis, a respectable surveyor, who died when David was only ten. He was a dutiful son who helped support his widowed mother and many siblings for some years after his father's death by working at various jobs near the family home outside of Bellefonte.

His career started to go afoul of the law after he enlisted in the Army of the United States before the War of 1812. However, he soon deserted and fled to Canada. Caught and awaiting hanging in Canada, the penalty during wartime, he managed his first of many daring escapes when the jail was set afire during the artillery bombardment from Fort Niagara, November 16-21, 1812. Now, as an outlaw, his wanderings, captures and escapes began. In Carlisle, he was caught, court-martialed, and quickly sentenced to death. As a result of his mother's intervention through the help of an old friend who was a judge, Lewis's sentence was commuted to life imprisonment and he was confined in the Carlisle guardhouse, his legs fettered by a ball and chain. Continuing a pattern he was to pursue thereafter, he somehow managed to escape by wriggling out of the irons, leaving the ball and chain behind. John Blair Linn, in *The History of Centre and Clinton Counties*, gives this improbable explanation:

> " . . . *his arms tapered from the shoulders to the ends of his fingers, his legs from the hips to the ends of his toes, so that it was almost impossible to keep manacles upon him. He could slip all ordinary handcuffs over his hands with ease, also over his ankles.*"

After eluding his pursuers from Carlisle, Lewis headed north. Following the scent of the trail of some excellent quality counterfeit notes to Burlington, Vermont, and armed with "a pair of wicked-looking horse-pistols," he headed back to Pennsylvania with a sack of crisp new bills. En route Lewis briefly befriended a General Root and easily swindled him out of a fine horse by paying him off with the bogus bills. Naturally, Lewis didn't dawdle, but quickly galloped on. The General innocently passed on some of the bills as payment for lodging in a nearby town where his fine reputation and upstanding character were unknown. He was summarily arrested as a counterfeiter. It was only after Root's identity was vouched for and his name cleared that a search party pursued, found and arrested Lewis in Troy, New York.

During this incarceration in Troy, David met his wife-to-be, Margaret, who later used the alias of Melinda, while he adopted the venerable Dutch name of Van Buren. This innocent young girl who lived across the street from the jail was captivated by the prisoner's sweet talk while he wooed her from his prison window. He managed to convince her that political enemies had wrongly put him behind bars. Melinda's friend, the jailer's daughter, helped arrange his escape and the couple eloped to Albany, New York. It was then on to New York City where Lewis carried out one of his most flamboyant robberies. He learned that Mrs. Jacob Astor, wife of the millionaire financier, would be attending a ladies auction sale. Having sent Melinda on ahead to Philadelphia, Lewis, dressed like a gentleman "in true dandy style," and some cohorts were on hand in the audience. They closely observed Mrs. Astor's every move and saw that the lady secreted her purchases of "rare laces and valuable pieces of jewelry" in her velvet reticule. Causing a momentary diversion, Lewis made off with her new treasures, which Mrs. Astor had carelessly left on a nearby bench. He went directly home and, as a loving gesture, gave Melinda a gift of lace that she only accepted on being assured that he had won it in a lottery. Later, when Lewis and

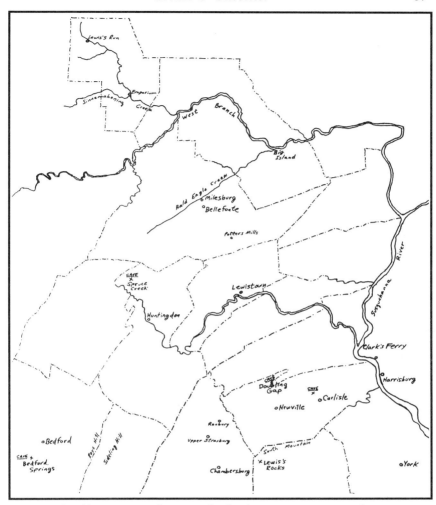

Map of Robber Country from Cumberland County History, *Vol. vi, No. 2, Winter 1989. Courtesy Cumberland County Historical Society, Carlisle, PA.*

his cronies were dividing up the loot they remembered the missing lace and accused and attacked him for holding out on them. It was time for Lewis to skip town once again.

Lewis's daring exploits frequently required new confederates and soon he and another band of counterfeiters and robbers ranged over a wide area, foraging northward as far as the Canadian border and New England, and westward to the Ohio River. The gang eventually narrowed its predatory range and Lewis settled near his mother's home northwest of Bellefonte, then and still the principal town in Centre

County. Possibly he came back to be close to his only baby daughter who was being cared for by his mother after Melinda's early, unexpected and deeply mourned death.

At this time his principal partner in crime, who is only referred to as "that man Connelly," seems to have been typecast as the heavy of the pair, "vicious, savage, and vindictive." The Carlisle *American Volunteer*, on December 30, 1819, describes him as:

> " . . . *about six feet high, not fleshy but weighs 230 or 40 pounds —with dark brown hair, little or no whiskers—rather long or lantern jaw'd—with a down look—an Irishman by birth, but speaks tolerably good English; though somewhat broad.*"

Lewis, his counterpart, had a mild manner, and "often restrained his companions in crime from excesses and murder," according to John Blair Linn. No corner of central Pennsylvania was safe, however, from the Lewis gang. On occasion they were said to hide out in caves. Along Route 45, the current owners of Indian Cave to the west, claim to have discovered traces of the gang's temporary retreat and "storehouse for their plunder," as well as relics and skeletons of Mohawk and Algonquin Indians. Between 1816 and 1820 the outlaws were guarded and fed by a family who lived near the cave. Nearby Woodward Cave also promotes itself as a Lewis gang hideout.

Desperate criminal though he was, Lewis was particularly gallant to the ladies. On more than one occasion the gang provided women travelers with safe escort over the Narrows, then and still a deserted stretch of mountain road separating Centre and Union counties. One male traveler, having heard of this weakness, took the precaution of dressing in women's clothes while carrying a substantial amount of money on a coach ride through the Narrows near Woodward, a known haunt of Lewis and Connelly. He was on his way to Pittsburgh to buy cattle. Unfortunately, the wily traveler forgot to shave. His disguise was easily discovered, and he was stripped of his clothes and cash when Lewis and his men waylaid his coach. They then tied him to a horse which was whipped into a gallop heading west, beyond the Narrows, where he was finally able to stop at the old stone tavern which was then and is today the Woodward Inn.

On another occasion Lewis approached a house on a prosperous looking farm with the intention of robbing its inhabitants. To find out where they kept their money, he asked the old woman who came to the door for change of five dollars. When she claimed she was a poor widow who didn't have a penny and was about to lose her only cow to the constable for unpaid rent, our so-called Robin Hood gave her the necessary 20 dollars, telling her to be sure to ask for a receipt. Hiding off the road that the constable was sure to take with the woman's payment, Lewis confronted him with drawn horse pistols and relieved his victim of the loan plus an additional 40 dollars, all the rest of the constable's money. That good deed, David was quoted as saying, was one of his best investments.

A colorful description of Lewis appears in a "Wanted" notice after another daring disappearance; it could as easily be a description of Robert Redford as the Sundance Kid.

Lewis did not head to Orleans or Kentucky, but back to his family on the Bennett branch of the Sinnemahoning River northwest of Bellefonte. Some time later, while nearing home after another escapade, a posse cornered and shot Lewis and Connelly. Connelly died the next day. But Lewis lingered on in the Bellefonte jail, weakened by an infected arm that turned gangrenous. He refused to have the arm amputated, and David Lewis died in jail on July 13, 1820 at the age of thirty-two.

During this last imprisonment, as he lay dying in his Bellefonte jail cell, Lewis is supposed to have written the *Confession or Narrative of David Lewis, the Robber and Counterfeiter,* a 37 page pamphlet revealing in florid detail his life of crime. John McFarland, editor of the *Carlisle Republican*, published it after his death. Despite its re-issuance as fact by C. D. Rishel as late as 1890, fastidious Centre County scholars W. Douglas Macneal and Gladys Murray doubt its authenticity today. They conclude that the "Confession" was written by McFarland himself in an attempt to discredit Governor William Findlay, his political adversary, who had apparently shown a lack of judgment by pardoning the scoundrel Lewis on September 3, 1819 after serving three and one half years of a six years sentence. One month later, on October 7th, an embarrassed Governor Findlay offered a $300 reward for Lewis and associates after the flagrant highway kidnapping and robbery of John McClelland, a wealthy Pittsburgh merchant. To make matters worse for Governor Findlay, Lewis was captured and managed to escape three more times over a six-month period. In the second escape, from the Bedford jail in December of 1819, he locked up the jailer and freed all but one of the other prisoners. The Governor actually visited Lewis in prison during one of his short stays. As McFarland sarcastically puts it:

300 Dollars Reward
ESCAPED from the jail of Bedford
County on Tuesday morning last,
DAVID LEWIS

Lately sentenced to imprisonment in the jail and penitentiary at
Philadelphia, for passing counterfeit notes.

The following is a description of his person:—Aged about 27 years,
six feet high, slim, straight, and well made. Rubby (sic) complexion,
large sandy whiskers, sandy or yellow hair cut in the fashion.
Genteel in his appearance, easy in his gait, polite in manners,
serious in his conversation and seldom seen to laugh.

Lewis has frequently visited the principal cities of the Union, and
has been long engaged in passing counterfeit money. He has passed
by names of Wilson, Philips, Green and Irwin, and once drove a
waggon between Baltimore and Charlestown, and according to his
own account, distributed upwards of $1000 of counterfeit paper in
the course of his trip. He has been in the army of the United States
from which he deserted; was frequently engaged, during the late
war, in robbing and plundering the American and British settlers on
the frontiers, where he is well known.

He has been frequently arrested and imprisoned upon criminal
charges and had uniformly effected his escape. It is probable that
he will make for Kentucky or Orleans, as it is understood Smith
and others of his fraternity have gone in that direction with a large
supply of counterfeit paper.

The manner of his escape from this prison of this county, is at
present the subject of legal investigation; and it is hoped that
whoever may have aided in it, will be brought to justice. In the
meantime, it is the duty, as well as the interest of every good citizen
to aid in his detection, for which the above reward will be paid.

Thomas Moore, Sheriff
Bedford, Pa.
February 29, 1816

THE
CONFESSION
OR
NARRATIVE,
OF
David Lewis.

———◦:◦:◦———

CONTAINING

An account of the Life and Adventures of this celebrated

COUNTERFEITER AND ROBBER,

From the commencement of his Career, until the period of his Death, in the Jail of Bellefonte, in consequence of a wound received in the attempt to retake him by the Posse Comitatus of Centre County.

———◦:✕:◦———

PRICE, FIFTY CENTS.

CARLISLE

PRINTED AND PUBLISHED BY

John M'Farland.

1820.

Title page from The Confession or Narrative of David Lewis. *Volume 20 No. 2*, Midwestern Folklore *Fall 1994. Courtesy Hoosier Folklore Society.*

"A visit from a Governor! and in jail too! Why the mere act itself was enough to inspire Lewis with new hopes, new life, and new resolution; and if the Governor did not lend him money and assistance or otherwise effect his escape, he read in the friendly demeanor of his distinguished visitor, at least a partial approbation of his deeds of crime and successful attempts at general jail delivery."

And again:

"Alas! We have fallen indeed upon evil times when the pardoning power of the Executive is thus ignorantly and improperly prostituted to the dangerous purpose of liberating infamous cut-throats, robbers and counterfeiters, for the sake of acquiring a short-lived popularity, or obtaining the reputation of a false humanity."

McFarland had lost his editorial post at the *Chambersburg Republican* two years earlier for opposing Findlay's first run for the governorship and apparently was still stung by the insult. If the theory of McFarland's fabrication of the "Confession" is true, his ploy in using it as a weapon against Findlay was certainly successful in capitalizing on the state's obvious mismanagement of prisons, since Governor Findlay was defeated for his second term. Even though Lewis died three months before the election, McFarland made capital of the "Confession" by publishing and widely distributing it in installments right up until Election Day. He arranged to have the printed pamphlet, priced at 50 cents, ready for distribution two weeks later, in the mode of today's hot-off-the-wire timely tell-it-all best sellers. An unplanned side effect of McFarland's efforts was to create an overblown impression of Lewis and his exploits to the public, and, in so doing, magnify and enhance the "noted robber" and Robin Hood legend.

Skeptics from Bellefonte at the time called the "Confession" "a FABRICATION, a collection of atrocious falsehoods." The Sheriff and Jailer of Centre County certified that Lewis made no confession, other than a verbal one to his minister, during his time in prison.

John Blair Linn comments:

"David Lewis was a remarkable man. Very pleasant and agreeable in social conversation and manners, of fine figure and physique, his features regular and beautiful, quite an Adonis. . . . Had he pursued a different course of life he might have been a valuable citizen."

And we wouldn't have nearly so interesting a story.

Chapter 7

Townspeople & Pageant

The Stovers

Nailed to the siding on the northwest corner of Stover's Village Store, in Aaronsburg, PA, is a small corroded bronze-colored plaque with the words "Geographic Center of Pennsylvania," half hidden by a large PEPSI cooler standing alongside its COCA COLA cousin. No one quite remembers when the sign was put there, but it was quite some time ago. Recall that the significance of the town's central location in Pennsylvania was one of the reasons that its founder, Aaron Levy, had great hopes for an expanding Aaronsburg community; that one day it would be the site preferred and selected for the new Pennsylvania state capital.

Today, adding to the impression of timelessness, many of the original log and frame houses still stand. Some of them are modified with Gothic porches and trim. Others are stripped down to the original bare chinked logs. Bruce Teeple tells me you can roughly date the age of a house by looking at the roofline. The roof's relation to the front door can determine its age. If the front door is under the low part of the roof, as is the case with most of the houses in town, that's a Georgian style of architecture and dates from before 1840. After 1840, the front door is under the peak of the roof and is considered Victorian. Teeple's is a log house built in 1838.

This postcard depicts the building that was Krapes Store until 1954. After 1954, it was owned and operated in succession by the Vonadas, the Greenlands, and finally, the Stovers. Courtesy Burt Stover.

Stover's Village Store, the only easily identifiable commercial enterprise among the set back comfortable private homes, sits on the crest of a hill plumb in the middle of town at Aaron's Square and Pine Street. The low part of its roofline parallels the front door. I remember Bruce Teeple telling me that a general store has existed on this site since 1802 when Polish refugee, Lyons Mussina, who is buried up at the Reformed cemetery, established it. It was Greenland's for many years until recently, when Burt and Colleen Stover bought it. Stover is a name that goes back in Haines Township at least eight generations, preceding by more than 30 years the founding of the town of Aaronsburg itself. But collateral connections among the Stovers today are hard to find. Next to Miller, Stover is the second most popular name in the area. Burt's branch of the family first settled further east in Mifflinburg and Lewisburg in Buffalo Valley. It was grandfather Miles (Mick) Stover who headed west over the Narrows to settle in Penns Valley. Burt says there were nine Stovers in Penns Valley Regional High School when he was a student there, and none of them could find any familial connection. Nor were any of them particularly interested.

It appears to me that curiosity for one's roots seems to come from not knowing. It's the outsiders who spend hours poring over old records and deeds in the Penns Valley Historical Association in Aaronsburg or the Centre County Historical Society in Bellefonte. Some are trying to find tenuous links with their past with dreams of noble heritage. And some, like me, stand in awe of a continuum of eight generations of Americans in a single town. My grandparents arrived in New York from the Ukraine 125 years ago. I would love to know something of our family history prior to that.

County records show that James Duncan was the first storekeeper in Aaronsburg, setting up shop in 1790, 12 years before Mussina. Born in Scotland in 1758, Duncan immigrated as a boy to Pennsylvania with his family who, in 1773, built a log cabin on the then existing narrow dirt road between the future Aaronsburg and Millheim. The Duncans retreated back to York County during the "Great Runaway." John Blair Linn, writing in 1883, recounts:

> *"James, having had some altercation with his father, wrapped his clothes in a handkerchief, had one of his brothers row him over the Rappahannock, and walked to Lewisburg, where he worked as a day laborer. His father wrote telling him to sell their tract of land, allowing him to keep all he received over fifty dollars. With this start Duncan went south along the Susquehanna to Northumberland, selected a small stock of goods which he could carry on horseback, and made his way back to Aaronsburg in the year 1790."*

He started out as a peddler, as have many successful merchants before they had the wherewithal to open permanent stores.

By 1798, the first Aaronsburg Post Office was established. It was housed in the store Duncan had opened, and Duncan was appointed postmaster. At some point, it became part of Lyons Mussina's store. Only recently, 200 years later during Greenland's reign, the post office was moved to a separate location, a block east on Aaron's Square.

Burt and Colleen use the space of the old post office, an alcove on the right as you enter, to display greeting cards. They've modernized the meat and produce area and plan on adding upright freezers soon. The tasteful sign outside reads, "Stover's Village Store, est. 1995, Snacks, Groceries, Quality Meats." A sensitive line drawing of a milk can on the left, and a wheat sheaf on the right, represent the principal produce in the valley.

Burt is tall, husky and round faced, with thick dark straight hair and a quiet smile. He came home to Aaronsburg after ten years in Colorado Springs to find new faces and voices he didn't know. He left behind a job he loved that paid well, but offered no retirement benefits. As head of design at a civil engineering firm, he was stressed with the pressure of deadlines. When he learned that Greenland's General Store was for sale back home in Aaronsburg, Burt saw a perfect opportunity to dig down into his family roots again. He was assured the store would practically run itself. Both he and Colleen agreed the job would be so easy, hence low pressured.

But after two years of 12-hour workdays (the store is open from 5:30 a.m. to 10:00 p.m., but Burt takes the afternoons off), the Stovers are finally coming up for air, and just about breaking even. Burt feels that at the age of 35 it's the kind of stress he can control, in a place he wants to be. At one point early on, to get some perspective, he sat down and wrote a poem listing his fears and grievances. That moment of introspection helped him get his bearings. He would tailor his store to fit the individual needs of his neighbors, and not try to compete with the big chains. The Stovers were certain by now that they could run the store well, and clear what they needed to live on. After all, the Greenlands put their seven kids through college this way, and the Stovers two were only 14 and 15 at the time we first met.

At the same time, Burt resolved to keep out of politics and not express his views on local issues, like the limestone mine, in a community split down the middle. Aaronsburg, he tells me, is known as "the town with those signs." "NIMBYs," do-gooders who declare "Not in my back yard!" have put up signs like "Too late, somebody's sold Penns Valley" along Route 45. Burt knows the issues, but he's almost mum as to his own feelings.

Since their arrival in the area, and until they could occupy the Porterfield home they bought in Millheim, Colleen and Burt had been living in Madisonburg over the ridge to the north in Brush Valley. In this part of the world, with its isolating ridge and valley topography, there is very little movement from one valley to the next. A road following Elk Creek, running south to north from Coburn to Brush Valley through Millheim, is one of the few natural breaks in the solid mountains. The consolidated schools, which draw from the communities of Woodward, Aaronsburg, Coburn, Millheim, Madisonburg and Rebersburg in both valleys, create a tenuous connection for students who still seem to cluster and center their friendships among their own neighbors. Madisonburg's old cemetery has totally different names on its tombstones from those in the Stover cemetery near Aaronsburg, and the current settlers are different, too. This would also be true in Nittany and Buffalo Valleys. Valley dwellers are very partisan about the specific place in which they live. Their neighbors in the adjacent valley are "foreigners." According to Peirce Lewis, who, as a geographer at Penn State should know, "people from the top of the Allegheny Front in Snowshoe and Clarence don't marry people from Nittany Valley at all; none, zero, zilch . . . and it's a distance of only twenty miles!"

A well stocked Stover's Village Store differs greatly from the basic items listed in the old ledgers in the Aaronsburg Museum. Today, they carry newspapers from as far afield as Pittsburgh, Philadelphia, Washington and New York. The video rental collection includes a selection probably not found in those urban centers, such as "Hunting the Elusive White Deer," and "Archery Strategies . . . How to Get Started." The shelves are stocked with corncob pipes, "Old Timer" knives, fishhooks, "Chore" gloves, emergency ponchos and "Silver Creek long cut smokeless tobacco" in wintergreen and cherry flavors. Magazines, candy, notions, canned goods and other staples, as well as top quality meat and produce, make Stovers much more than your typical minimart.

A sign left over from Greenland's near the front of the store reads, "No credit, no exceptions." But Burt soon found out that his customers expected not only credit, but conversation and check cashing, too. This included cashing unemployment and welfare checks and accepting food stamps. He now calls his establishment The Last National Bank of Aaronsburg. Customers come in with a check to pay their bills, and then ask him to hold it a spell, not deposit it right away. For some of his Nebraska Amish customers, he even has to write their checks. With only a basic education many of them can't spell. Burt's the banker, and Colleen sometimes finds herself an unofficial doctor for their Amish customers, answering medical questions and prescribing over-the-counter remedies for fever and runny noses. The Amish have much the same buying habits as his other customers, including condoms from the vending machine in the men's room.

The Amish, who are making a strong presence in eastern Centre County, are, as John A. Hostetler puts it in *Amish Society,*

> "*. . . a church, a community, a spiritual union, a conservative branch of Christianity, a religion, a community whose members practice simple and austere living, a familistic entrepreneuring system, and an adaptive human community.*"

They consider all members equal, and they do not take part in "worldly" government, swear oaths, or participate in war. Burt Stover finds the Nebraska Amish in Penns Valley, a misnomer since they come from Ohio, strange in comparison to the Lancaster Amish from eastern Pennsylvania, who have settled near his Madisonburg house. His neighbors there are wealthy, well groomed, well dressed, industrious, very religious and totally abstemious, as far as liquor and tobacco are concerned. Farming is their principal occupation. Although maintaining a tight community, they move more in the world by having established successful businesses, such as a harness shop, bakery and plant nursery, which are patronized as well by "English," a term the Amish use for "usns." People come from all over to the harness shop that sells a popular brand of work shoes. In fact, the area around Madisonburg is known as "Little Lancaster," after the well-known community to the southeast.

The Nebraska Amish in Penns Valley, who mainly run sawmills or operate dairy farms, are poorer and live marginally, selling milk and wood for cash, and bartering for other necessities. The women frequently do quilting piecework to add to their meager income. They adhere more rigidly to separation from the contemporary world that surrounds them. However, they are more liberal with their children, who have a four-year period, from 14 to 18, when they can choose whether to follow their parents' religion and way of life. Once they've chosen, they must stay or face "shunning," a total ostracism from family and the Amish community.

Saturday night is gathering time for young Amish males at Stover's Village Store. One is apt to see as many as eight spindly buggies parked in front, with square white tops and red triangle reflectors highlighted in ghostly fashion in the dark night. Their owners, faces shaded by broad-brimmed hats, sit or squat outside, drinking coffee, smoking and chewing tobacco, until closing time at nine. That's about as much of a gathering place as you'll find in Aaronsburg. Retirees used to hang out around the post office, but the postmaster put a stop to it. The churches, Stover's Village Store, the post office, and a coffee shop at the edge of town, are all there is. Outside of the Fall Festival, the library plant sale and the museum's Valley Games, Aaronsburgers don't seem to put much store in congregating.

Musicks and Mingles

> *'The more sedentary browsers' can be compared with the 'brainier migratory grazers. And sedentary species, like sedentary genes, are terribly successful for a while, but in the end they are self-destructive.'*
>
> Dr. Elizabeth Vrba, paleontologist from Pretoria, quoted by Bruce Chatwin in *Songlines*.

Ralph Musick was born on a farm in Aaronsburg, and has never left home. He's a trim man, squeaky clean, with grey hair, high color and glasses. Like Randall Stover, his neighbor, Ralph stayed on the family farm to help his father during World War II. In order to keep farms sufficiently manned to produce the food needed for the war effort, the Selective Service had devised a system of furloughing for farmers, so many units credit for the number of acres or head of cattle. His father had enough units to furlough Ralph, but not enough for his older brother, who was then hired out to another farmer, who furloughed him. So both brothers did their patriotic duty by staying at home in Penns Valley.

"I was a farm boy all my life," he tells me proudly. His parents farmed the Meyers' acreage, site of Hosterman's Pit and a future limestone mine, for 27 years while it was a 'steel farm.' They sold out in 1955 to an Amish family and moved into Aaronsburg proper, a fairly typical pattern for aging farmers, particularly with the Amish moving up from Kishacoquillas Valley, one valley over to the south, so eager to buy farmland to distribute to their numerous offspring. Most Aaronsburg town lots, which are long and narrow, have a barn or other outbuildings behind the main house so that farmers, who moved into town, could still keep a few animals.

Musick's father was first generation in Penns Valley. "I'm not a historian," Ralph asserts. "Our name is possibly German." A clue, he surmises, is that his parents, like the Amish, spoke Pennsylvania Dutch. "I admire Amish. We get along," he acknowledges. But for Musick they speak too fast and are hard to understand. As neighbors on the farm, they depended on him for chores their religion disallows. But they always returned the favor. One time, he recalls, he got a call from an Amish neighbor, Dave Yoder, asking to be picked up at a hospital in Lewisburg, since Ralph had a car and his neighbor only his horse and buggy. A few days later he found Yoder out in the field mending the Musick's fence, without his ever having asked.

Ralph retired in 1991 as an "incubator operator" for the Agriculture College at Penn State. His work was with chickens, turkeys, pheasants, grouse and quail. Once he tried hatching an ostrich egg, he tells me, but it didn't work. "Maybe there wasn't enough humidity," muses Ralph, "or maybe it was an old egg."

Ralph has been unusually active in the Aaronsburg community, serving on the boards of the Civic Club and the museum. His many other civic hats include auditor of the Water Board, school director, chaplain of the Masonic Lodge, and treasurer of the Salem Evangelical Lutheran Church. He sings in its choir, too. His activities even spill over to the adjacent town of Millheim, one mile away, where he served as treasurer of the Lions Club.

Mrs. Musick, Ardranna, is the daughter of Abner (Abby/Al) Mingle who was a moving spirit in the Aaronsburg Story event in 1949. Wary, cautious, trim-cut brown hair, she sports short shorts this summer's day. Their house, at the time we met, was on the western end of town on Aaron's Square, and was converted from a Mobil gas station and pool-room in 1962. They still had the original hardwood floors. Out back were the three Musick's Cottages, then the only overnight facilities in Aaronsburg, save for two fancy Bed and Breakfasts run by "newcomers." Aaronsburg, the Musicks say confidently, is a "nice little town." The people who come from all over and stay in the cottages "tell us what's here."

The Aaronsburg Pageant

Abby Mingle, Ardranna's father, whose grandfather's grandfather actually knew Aaron Levy, was sitting on his porch on a spring day in 1949 when the writer Arthur Lewis stopped to talk. Mingle lived on the main drag, Route 45, as it wends its way through Aaronsburg. According to Ardranna, "My dad set on the porch a lot," commenting on his meeting with Lewis. Lewis, later the author of *The Aaronsburg Story*, read the sign "Aaronsburg, founded by Aaron Levy in 1786" while driving through town and stopped and questioned Mingle. Lewis was intrigued with what he heard. Not just because Levy was an orthodox Jew who, in laying out the town set aside choice land for the German churches, burial grounds and a school. Other town planners had done as much. Rather, Lewis was fascinated by Levy's presentation of a pewter communion set to the congregations. As a result of this serendipitous encounter Lewis, who happened to be Jewish and was an advance man for Pennsylvania's Governor James H. Duff, dreamed up the idea of creating an event around the 150th anniversary of the first services at Aaronsburg's Salem Evangelical Lutheran Church in 1799. Its purpose was to promote brotherhood and ecumenism in Pennsylvania during Brotherhood Week; and incidentally, to boost the image of his boss, the Governor.

Intrigued at his notion of a commemorative event, Lewis returned to Aaronsburg the next day and visited Reverend James Shannon, then minister of the Salem Evangelical Lutheran Church, who filled in background details on the town's founding. Shannon reverentially and ceremoniously showed Lewis the communion set designed by Colonel William Will of Philadelphia, "the best 18th century pewterer in America." Arthur Lewis's promoter's imagination took flight and the rest is history. On October 23rd that year, an historical pageant involving over 30,000 participants and spectators took place in a natural amphitheater on the edge of Aaronsburg, a quiet town of 680 inhabitants, . . . "The Aaronsburg Story."

"Call A. E. Mingle for dependable Insurance and Bonds, Notary Public." That was Abby's ad in the State College *Centre Daily Times*. His job was insurance, but somehow Abby Mingle became president of the Aaronsburg project. He wasn't in the pageant, but, according to Ardranna, he "worked his butt off." "He went and done it. He kept us pumped up." Her father always had some juicy bit to tell his family. There were dinners in Philadelphia, endless committee meetings, and heady activity for a small-town gent. He took it all to heart. Not her mother. It was "not her tray of cookies," says Ardranna. "I was so sick of it," she remarks, with a pained expression on her otherwise bland face.

The Musicks were living on their farm then. It was only when they saw all the people come they "knew it was special." They ate lunch with celebrities. They don't remember who they were right now. The celebrities impressed the Musicks the most. "Them people in that category are the most common people," Ralph intones. "The Aaronsburg Story was the greatest celebration this town witnessed." After 1949, some new people arrived. Before that he could name every person in town. As for her father, Ardranna says he was an "unlicensed lawyer." He helped everybody with wills and other problems. "Ralph's a little like him. Everybody leans on you."

Living and Dramatizing Penn and Levy's Dream

Sunday, October 23, 1949 was an exhilarating day for Doris Mamolen. She was in her glory. A storm, which threatened to dampen the pageant, had cleared, and throngs of people from Penns Valley and beyond were crowding the natural outdoor amphitheater. Movie star Cornel Wilde, who came from Hollywood to narrate the pageant of the Aaronsburg Story before an estimated crowd of from 30,000 to 50,000 people, turned to her, standing next to him on the outdoor platform and said, as she remembers it, "The lovely colors of autumn are in your cheeks." Wilde was the principal point of interest, then and now, for most of the local attendees, far outweighing the distinguished international guests, thought provoking panel discussions on brotherhood, or the story of

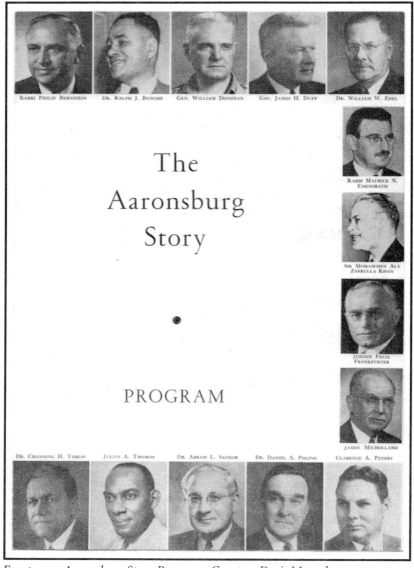

Front cover Aaronsburg Story Program. Courtesy Doris Mamolen.

pioneer Aaron Levy. The overall theme was the hope that man could overcome his prejudice of race and religion and join together in brotherhood.

Distinguished international leaders, who represented a cross-section of races and religions, took part in panel discussions. They

COMMEMORATION PROGRAM

Centre County's Share in the State-Wide Observance of
"Pennsylvania Week"

AARONSBURG, PENNSYLVANIA
October 23, 1949

"The history of Aaronsburg typifies what this nation
and the world are trying to do in erasing intolerance
of religion, race, and color."—Governor James H. Duff

8:45 A.M. WORSHIP SERVICE—Salem Lutheran Church

Speaker—Dr. Frederick Keller Stamm, Former Pastor, First Congregational
Church, Chicago, Illinois

Rabbi Philip S. Bernstein, Vice-President of Central Conference of
American Rabbis, Rochester, N. Y.

**10:00 A.M. PUBLIC MEETING DEDICATED TO RELIGIOUS AND RACIAL UN-
DERSTANDING** (Pageant Site)

Co-Chairman, Dr. J. W. Claudy, Aaronsburg Story Committee

Presiding—Honorable James H. Duff, Governor of Pennsylvania

Dr. Daniel A. Poling, Editor, The Christian Herald

Honorable Felix Frankfurter, Associate Justice, United States Supreme Court

Dr. Ralph J. Bunche, Former Mediator, United Nations Palestine
Commission

General William J. Donovan, Former Director, Office of Strategic
Services

11:00 A.M. BROTHERHOOD INSTITUTES (Held simultaneously)

Chairman—Mr. Clarence A. Peters, Director, Northeastern Division, National
Conference of Christians and Jews

NUMBER 1—Salem Lutheran Church

"Techniques of Handling Prejudice and Prejudiced People"

Coordinator—Mr. Clarence Zorger, Superintendent of Schools, Harrisburg,
Pennsylvania

Resource Speaker—Rabbi Maurice N. Eisendrath, President, The Union
of American Hebrew Congregations

Panel Speakers:

Rabbi Philip D. Bookstaber, Temple Ohev Shalom, Harrisburg, Pa.

Dr. Andrew Gottschall, Philadelphia Director, National Conference of
Christians and Jews

Mrs. Myra Blakeslee—Director of Education, Division Against Discrimination, State of New Jersey

Mr. Julius Thomas, Director, National Urban League

General William J. Donovan, Former Director, Office of Strategic Services

The Aaronsburg Story Commemoration Program. Courtesy Doris Mamolen.

included United States Supreme Court Justice Felix Frankfurter; Dr.
Ralph Bunche, former Mediator of the United Nations Palestine Com-
mission; Sir Mohammed Aly Z. Khan, vice-president of the United
Nations General Assembly and Minister of Foreign Affairs of Pakistan;
James H. Duff, Governor of Pennsylvania; General William J. Dono-
van, former Director of the Office of Strategic Services; and Dr. Daniel

NUMBER 2—Evangelical and Reformed Church
"Religious Intolerance and American Society"
Coordinator—Dr. William Edel, President, Dickinson College
Resource Speaker—Dr. Abram L. Sachar, President, Brandeis University
Panel Speakers:

Mr. Maurice Fagan—Director, Fellowship Commission, Philadelphia, Pa.

Sir Mohammed Aly Zafrulla Khan, Vice-President of the United Nations General Assembly, and Minister of Foreign Affairs, Commonwealth Relations, Government of Pakistan.

Mr. Allyn P. Robinson, Director, Commission on Religious Organizations, National Conference of Christians and Jews

Mr. John Sullivan, Director of Education and Public Relations, New York State Commission Against Discrimination

Dr. Frederick Keller Stamm, Former Pastor, First Congregational Church, Chicago, Illinois

Rabbi D. A. Jessurun Cardozo, Mikveh Israel Synagogue, Philadelphia, Pa.

NUMBER 3—Evangelical United Brethren Church
"How to Assure Minority Groups Their Rights and Dignities as Americans"
Coordinator—Mr. James Milholland, Acting President, Pennsylvania State College
Resource Speaker—Dr. Charles S. Johnson, President, Fisk University

Panel Speakers:

Mr. J. Harold Saks, Community Services Director, Anti-Defamation League of B'nai B'rith

Mr. Russell Bradley, Pittsburgh Director, National Conference of Christians and Jews

Rabbi Philip S. Bernstein, Vice-President of Central Conference of American Rabbis

Dr. Channing H. Tobias, Director, Phelps-Stokes Foundation

Miss Marjorie Penny, Director, Fellowship House, Philadelphia, Pa.

12:30 P.M. **LUNCH**

2:00 P.M. **OPEN AIR HISTORICAL PAGEANT**—"The Issue Of An Ideal."

5:00 to
6:00 P.M. **SYMPOSIUM**—Brotherhood for Peace and Freedom—Salem Lutheran Church

Presiding—Honorable James H. Duff, Governor of Pennsylvania

Sir Mohammed Aly Zafrulla Khan, Vice-President of the United Nations General Assembly, and Minister of Foreign Affairs, Commonwealth Relations, Government of Pakistan

Dr. Abram L. Sachar, President, Brandeis University

Dr. Channing H. Tobias, Director, Phelps-Stokes Foundation

Presented by the Commonwealth of Pennsylvania in cooperation with the
National Conference of Christians and Jews
Federal Council of Churches of Christ in America
Anti-Defamation League of B'nai B'rith
Historical Society of Pennsylvania
The Pennsylvania State College
B'nai B'rith Hillel Foundation of America
Centre County Public Schools
Centre County Granges and Affiliates
Centre County Veterans Organizations

The Aaronsburg Story Commemoration Program. Courtesy Doris Mamolen.

Poling, Editor of *The Christian Herald*. They talked about Religious Intolerance and American Society; Techniques of Handling Prejudice and Prejudiced People, and How to Assure Minority Groups Their Rights and Dignities as Americans. *Life* magazine, *The New York Times*, *CBS*, all covered Aaron Levy's day in the sun.

The celebrations closed with benedictions and a 30,000 voice chorus singing "America the Beautiful." Then the day was over and Aaronsburg went back to its old ways. Not one Jew, nor black, nor hardly any Catholics, have ever lived in Aaronsburg proper, but it and Aaron Levy had achieved, if not immortality, much more than 15 minutes of fame.

Today, a tiny, dynamic, white-wavy-haired, blue-eyed widow of 88, bent over by the years, Doris Mamolen looks back with clarity to that morning when she must have been a stunning 38 year old. Fifty years later she still glows at the memory.

At the time of the Aaronsburg Story, Doris was a fairly recent arrival in Penns Valley. She had moved from Philadelphia as a newlywed after having served as Captain Doris Brill in the WACs during World War II. Her husband was widower Morris Mamolen who ran Nieman's clothing store in Millheim, founded by his first wife's father, David J. Nieman in 1908. Nieman came from Lock Haven, one of a number of Lithuanian Jewish immigrants whom Harris Claster, an enterprising businessman and earlier arrival, supplied with goods. As itinerant peddlers they drove their wagons from farm to farm through north central Pennsyl-

In 1910, the Nieman building housed Nieman's store (left) and the Millheim Banking Company. Davy Nieman and Harry Mensch stand at left, and bank employees S. Ward Gramley, P. H. Musser, and D. Zerby at right. The store eventually expanded into the entire building. Millheim, Millheim Bicentennial Magazine, p.85, 1988, Courtesy Penns Valley Historical Association.

vania, selling pots and sewing supplies and sweets to eager, isolated farm families. Claster, who also arranged their ocean passage, went on to establish a large building supply company. And many of those ped-dlers' wagons grew into substantial small town department stores, like Nieman's.

"The whole valley was in on it," Doris says, meaning the preparation for the forums and pageant held on the natural sloping amphitheater on the northeast corner of the village of Aaronsburg. Penn State, with the wholehearted support of its then president, Milton Stover Eisen-hower (brother of the future President), helped with the major logis-tics and publicity. Dr. W. R. Gordon, a professor of Rural Sociology, wrote "The Issue of an Ideal," the text for the pageant. The University Drama department designed the sets and costumes, which were con-structed and sewn by willing helpers throughout Penns Valley, who also appeared in the tableaux as settlers and Indians. "It was a wonderful affair. Too bad! Those things don't last too long," Doris says wistfully.

But the spirit of tolerance and brotherly love extolled by Justice Frankfurter, Sir Mohammed Aly Khan, Dr. Ralph Bunche, and other world figures at seminars prior to the pageant, was actually being lived every day by Doris and her husband. They were the only Jewish residents within a 23-mile radius in Penns Valley at the time. The Mamolens occupied a four-bedroom apartment over Nieman's store in the heart of Millheim, one mile west of Aaronsburg, along Route 45. Although small, Millheim was a market town, the hub, a place to go, drawing families from Coburn and Brush Valley as well as Aaronsburg. Especially on Saturday nights. That's when the stores stayed open late and farmers came to town to socialize and shop. Morris was always very accommodating to his customers. He stocked a first class line of mens-wear and would special order anything they wanted. He was known to have bragged, "I buried more Hart Schaffner and Marx suits than anyone else around!" Many of his farmer customers wanted to go out in style.

On her first Saturday night in Millheim, Doris was startled by such a hubbub in the street below that she thought there was a fire. It was just the usual Saturday night crowd milling around outside the store and letting off steam. Nieman's was located in the center of town, at Penn and East Main Streets, the juncture of Routes 45 and 445, across the street from the bank and diagonally across from Hosterman and Stover's hardware store that served as another focal point. It was like a

Saturday night *passegiatta* one finds in small Italian towns where families would stroll and young girls arm in arm giggle among themselves at the looks of prospective boy friends.

Aaronsburg, situated just one mile east of Millheim, was too small to accept diversity, Doris feels, despite the wishes of its founder. "It takes small children, a cat or a dog to integrate into a community," says Doris who had none of the above. Millheim offered more opportunities. It was a viable town, with mills harnessing the waterpower from Elk Creek, which ran through it, unlike Aaronsburg which was arbitrarily subdivided on a map with no justification for legitimacy, other than its supposed central location.

Today, Doris lives in State College. Hosterman and Stover's hardware store has been replaced by the Post Office, the owners having relocated west of Millheim on Route 45. Nieman's is boarded shut and the funeral parlor and barber and jewelry store, the electrician and drugstore are gone, too. And on Saturday nights the hub is quiet. Nowadays farmers stay home and watch television or hang out at the mall.

Levy's Gift

I have made a special appointment for Ralph Musick to show me the communion set. He disappears into a back room of the former Mobil station and, with due ceremony, produces a sturdy brass-trimmed mahogany box, opens it with a silent "ta da!" and lets me handle the contents. The set consists of a paten, chalice, cruet and flagon. At about ten inches tall, they are larger than I had expected. A muted luster attests to their age. I turn the flagon over to reveal William Will's mark of two circles that enclose two eagles. It feels smooth and warm to the touch. "Das Geschenke Zudenen Deutschen Gemeinden in Arensberg (sic) Von Aron Levy" is the inscription. "This gift to the German Churches of Aaronsburg by Aaron Levy." Myth has it that Levy walked down the aisle during the inaugural service, presented his gift to the minister, and left. It was obviously Levy's intent to make his gift to all the Christian congregations of the town. But Salem Lutheran Church papers recorded the gift, and it was used as part of the church's communion service until before the Civil War.

After that the set's whereabouts was unknown until D. Sparr Wert found it under the pulpit during a remodeling of the church in 1914. Wert was 24 at the time, a member of the congregation, a farmer and a carpenter. Some of the elders wanted to sell the pewter set. When

Wert demurred, they gave it to him for safekeeping. He kept it for many years, and finally, in 1933, enlisted cabinetmaker John Haines to fashion a cabinet out of some fine black walnut Wert had cut down on his farm. He then cut an opening in a brick wall of the church, and installed a glass door with a lock. That was where the communion set was housed when Rev. Shannon showed it to Arthur Lewis.

Ten years later, in 1959, the church burned down. The communion set survived and thereafter was kept "in barns and odd places" until its significance and value was recognized by outsiders.

After the fire, Fred McLaughlin, a church member, made the presentation box in which it is now kept. The box and its contents vanished from public view, only to be brought out by Ralph Musick on special occasions, like the 200th anniversary of the laying of the cornerstone of the original Salem Church in 1994. Ralph won't say where the box is stored. It is obviously too big for a bank deposit vault. He is adamant that they will never lend it. "We might sound selfish. New York put on a show and they said, 'We'll insure it for a million dollars.' "What's a million dollars, I say, if it's gone? This set has a lot of meaning for our church."

The author and Pennsylvania State Representative Kerry Benninghoff with the Levy communion set. Photo by Michelle Klein, Centre Daily Times.

According to Bruce Teeple, the museum in Aaronsburg would love to house the town's most valuable historic asset. Musick also has the original town map, which he keeps folded: "bad" for preservation. Unsaid is the fact that the little museum is not secure enough, nor does it have the appropriate place to house town "treasures." A campaign to build a combined regional museum and library on the site of the Aaronsburg Story is underway. Maybe, when there's a proper depository, all Aaronsburg's treasures will be brought together.

It was outsiders who, over the course of time, have made Aaronsburg aware of itself, starting with Aaron Levy. Then it was Arthur Lewis who opened the townspeople's eyes to their place in history through his dramatization of *The Aaronsburg Story*. Today it is outsiders who practice organic farming, who work in State College, or who have opened small businesses like Bed & Breakfasts and potteries, who demand a reten-

Scenes from The Issue of an Ideal *presented at the Aaronsburg Story Pageant. Scenes were narrated and silently acted out by townspeople. Courtesy Centre County Historical Society.*

tion of the quality of life they sought and thought they had found in this tiny out-of-the-way, in the middle-of-nowhere, free-from-pollution town. Townsfolk are mainly passive, particularly those former farmers who, in the main, have sold their farms to Amish from the Big Valley, or Kishacoquillas and have retired to one of Levy's lots in town. In 1949 they ignored, then tolerated, then finally joined the pageant.

Chapter 8

THE MOUNTAIN MAN & THE MINER

It's fascinating how two people can be faced with the same facts yet arrive at radically different conclusions. Likewise, two people can share a similar background and history and grow up in a similar locale, yet have utterly opposing viewpoints on what is best for that locale.

The Mountain Man

Talk about a sense of place, Randall Stover has it. He knows Penns Valley inside out, from the rolling farmland to the clear trout streams to the hunters' remote woodlands. He has farmed, fished and hunted the land all his life and claims there's no place he'd rather be. His roots spread wide and deep, back to the original 1780s settler families—Stover, Hosterman and Motz who migrated to this limestone valley in Central Pennsylvania, so like their beloved Palatinate in southern Germany. Most of Randall's folks worked as hard in this new land as their ancestors did in the Palatine.

Randall's Grandfather Motz owned woodland. He cut first growth pine logs as long as 84 feet which were taken by horse and wagon to Coburn to be shipped by rail. Coburn boasted the only nearby railroad stop of the Lewisburg and Tyrone Railroad, a branch of the Pennsylvania Railroad. It served an area including Woodward, Aaronsburg, Millheim in Penns Valley and Rebersburg and Madisonburg in Brush Valley. One time called "The Forks," Coburn was the point of confluence of Penns, Elk and Pine Creeks, the principal source of water and transportation. Earlier, before the railroad was built, lumber and other goods were sent by raft down Penns Creek in spring when the water level was high.

Great-grandfather Georgie Stover was also a woodsman, an excellent carpenter making cabinets and coffins and other necessaries in Woodward. Randall is the first Stover since then to follow in his great-grandfather's steps. He has always been creative with his hands, as an electrician, plumber, carpenter and cabinetmaker, all self-taught except for one shop class in high school. For his own pleasure nowadays Randall works in wood, making furniture, clock cases, antiques copies, toys, puzzles, sight-gags and gimmicks like his "quarter-pounder" (which pounds a real quarter), and his "tax shelter" (made of thumb tacks.)

But Randall is serious about the quality of any job he tackles. "I do the old hand styling and dovetailing. No jigs or routers. I cut 'em by hand," he tells me. He uses no patterns. Bruce Teeple calls him a "native genius." It's all in his head, Randall explains. "I make 'em and then I give 'em away," he boasts to me, although he wouldn't turn down an offer of a sale. Randall is proud of his three-foot elephant and donkey with reflector eyes to be displayed at the Woodward Festival. He hauls them out of the back of his workshop for me to see. There's already a customer waiting to add them to his front lawn menagerie in Woodward.

Randall's latest project is a small tabernacle for the chapel at St. Mark's Catholic High School in Wilmington, Delaware where his only child, Dave, teaches science. A "book boy," 42-year-old Dave is married and has a Ph.D. in nuclear physics, a first in the Stover clan. Whenever Dave comes back home to Aaronsburg, he spends time at the museum with his friend, Bruce Teeple. They share enlarged curiosities, and roam the area scouting for fossils.

Randall caresses the plane-smoothed black oak of the tabernacle as he talks of his plans to create a cross out of dogwood, the wood used for the "true cross," I am told. The items Randall donates to the annual Woodward Fall Festival usually fetch the highest prices at auction. He gives the festival of his time and physical energy too, by helping out with the traditional pig roast, working almost 12 hours preparing this year's 600-pound porker.

Now 81 and retired, with activity limited by four fused discs in his lower back and an artificial knee, Randall leans on his cane and reflects through clouded blue eyes on a hardworking life spent entirely in and around the eastern end of Penns Valley, along Route 45. More than slightly paunchy, "all muscle," he claims, with the ruddy complexion of an outdoorsman, sporting a grey baseball cap indoors over his thin grey hair, he sits at his kitchen table. Tapping his stubby fingers rhythmically, he reaches back in time a bit ruefully to World War II when he was the last of the four Stover boys left on the farm.

Randall was drafted like the rest, passed his physical and was about to ship out from Harrisburg when, as he tells it, he was yanked out of line at the last moment by a member of the draft board and sent back to his father's farm. It was government policy, they claimed. One Stover boy had to stay home and help make food for "the boys who were going."

So, like Ralph Musick and many others, he stayed put. His twin brother, Russell went off to war and, in the Normandy invasion, was the first man to set up a machine gun that didn't get knocked out by German artillery on Omaha Beach. Even though he was wounded shortly after D Day, Russell caught the traveling bug and has been making it his business to try to see the rest of the world ever since. The G.I Bill was Russell's ticket to more education and a white-collar job. Until he retired, he was a loan officer at the People's Bank in Millheim.

Randall, who lacked his brother's ticket, has made a few forays around the country, and still talks vaguely of distant travel. Economics, his own and his wife Gladys's health, plus the reality that he hasn't ventured forth so far, make his leaving Penns Valley now quite unlikely.

From as far back as he can remember Randall has worked hard, starting at the family farm on Middle Road in Woodward, right next to the cemetery. His parents, speaking Pennsylvania Dutch when they were married at 23, were very much like the Amish families who have been buying out many of the farms in the valley today. "Grandpa Motz, he spoke Pennsylvania Dutch to us boys as we grew up. He could speak English, but Pennsylvania Dutch came the easiest to him. We know it, we understand it, but we can't talk it. We grew up exactly like the Amish," he informs me. It took until 1939 for the Stover's farm to finally get electrified. When Amish families buy farms today they remove all those extraneous wires.

Randall's earliest chore as a boy was gathering eggs from the hen house on the farm in Woodward. As soon as he and his brothers grew stronger and learned how, they took on other jobs. The boys put down bedding, fed the animals, cut weeds and split wood. Every year they planted four rotation cash crops: wheat, hay, corn, and oats, which the Stovers farmed with a team of horses. They had five horses in all, for driving and buggy riding. In addition there were 500 chickens and 50 to 60 hogs to tend to and butcher. Twenty-five of their 80 acres were pastureland for anywhere from 8 to 35 head of cattle during the war years. Farm work occupied 18 out of 24 hours every day, he tells me. And with all this labor one couldn't say the Stover family flourished. They produced only enough to live on, with no surplus.

By the time he was fully grown, Randall, as in the story of the boy and the calf, routinely hauled as much as 120 pound bags of feed and fertilizer over his shoulder. "We were tough. We grew up tough. I done all the tractor work, all the chopping work, all the heavy lifting." Some years later, while making necessary adjustments to his toil-worn body, a lady "choirpractor" told Randall Stover "You're just a little mule trying to do a big horse's work."

For Randall, taking care of the farm was his responsibility during World War II. If he had his druthers when the war was over, he wouldn't have remained. His dream was to become a forester. But that would have required further schooling. He dutifully stayed on with his parents until they sold the Woodward property to an Amish family in 1948 and retired to a house in Aaronsburg. That was the pattern of many retired farmers.

Gladys Shawver, to whom Randall was engaged way back when the farm was sold, was frail even then, not strong enough for the rigors of farm life. Her early life had been hard. Her sister had to quit school and go to work when she was eleven. Gladys and Randall were lucky to have finished 12th grade. They courted for ten years. "She had a hard time tying me down, I guess," he says with a weary twinkle as she smiles back, rocking slowly in her Lazyboy chair. Gladys appears calm and nods and smiles as he talks, slightly removed from our circle around the table in the cheerful kitchen he designed and built for her. She is small and slim, and neatly dressed, with a pretty heart-shaped face and upturned nose. Her pallor is undoubtedly the result of two open-heart operations. She sleeps or dozes 70 percent of the time, according to Randall, and finds solace in music.

God made the mountains
And the Valleys
And all of the trees.
And God made me
A Mountain Man
I am a Mountain Man
This is where I am the closest
And walk and talk with my Lord
When the gentle breeze
Blows through the needles
Of the White Pine Tree
My Lord is whispering to me
When the wind rustles the leaves
Of the mighty White Oak Tree
He is speaking to me
When storm winds roar
Over the mountain top
My Lord is calling me to attention
When the Wild Turkey calls I answer
And it comes to me
I call to my Lord
He answers and is with me
The Pileate Woodpecker
Drills a hole in a tree for food
It reminds me
My Lord is knocking on my heart
To let him come in
The Great Horned Owl
Calls to his mate
She answers
And he comes to her
When I kill a deer or turkey for food
I look down at it
And am sorry for I have killed
One of God's most beautiful creatures
Then I get down on my knees
And I look to the heavens above
And say
Thank you Lord
I am a Mountain Man.

Randall Stover

Obviously he needed to focus on how to earn a living after the farm was sold. With no credentials other than farm labor, wherever he went looking for work he was turned down. Even then he was skilled with his hands and a quick study. "I was not a veteran," Randall says gravely. "I couldn't get a job." "A good job," his wife Gladys echoes as she nods and rocks. In the deeply grooved fibers of their marriage Gladys's role is one of the uncomplaining quiet invalid reinforcing her husband's healthy ego. But get her alone and she quickly and clearly speaks her own mind, and with wit.

After the war, just as before, there was no industry in the valley. Only farms and small family businesses. Woodward had a population of around 250. Since it was founded in 1786 by Randall's great-great Grandfather, Jacob Motz, there was an inn, a bank, a post office, a school, two churches, three blacksmiths, a barber-dentist, a doctor, a shoemaker, a bakery, a cider press and several stores; today just the inn and a general store/post office remain. Aaronsburg, the next town heading west along Route 45, had more inhabitants, but no industries. Millheim, the next community, just one mile west of Aaronsburg, which was a regular small town boasting a bank, clothing store, hardware store and hotel, plus other necessaries, had nothing to offer Randall.

Eventually he found work with the Bethlehem Steel Company mining limestone in nearby Naginey. All these years later, sitting in his comfortable kitchen, Randall still winces at the memory of the pervasive stone dust and the noise to which he was exposed every working day.

When water problems halted mining at Naginey, Bethlehem transferred Randall back home to Aaronsburg to refurbish the so-called "steel" farms the company owned in the surrounding countryside. He and a crew improved the properties by installing furnaces, bathrooms and kitchens; building chicken houses, hog pens, rebuilding barns, and drilling wells. The land was then leased to and cultivated by local farmers.

Mustering his many practical skills, once his new job was assured, Randall built their snug house on Plum Street in Aaronsburg. He drew the plans on a piece of plywood, marked the best pine and hemlocks on his family's hundred acres of timberland on Roundtop Mountain, then hired lumbermen to fell and haul the logs to the mill where they were sawed into 2 x 6 inch boards. "When we were done building we only had 6 left over, and ten boards. Figured it all," he says with satisfaction. Gladys adds for emphasis, "The kitchen, he built the kitchen." The cabinets are expertly crafted of knotty pine. Around the living room Randall shows me where he has used butternut, walnut and cherry as well. He keeps all these native woods stockpiled in his fastidious garage workshop behind the house.

The Stover family's 100 woodland acres have been pretty well lumbered off by now. The last cut had big timber, 42 to 44 inches across. The brothers sold only the timber, not the land. "Oh, no. We're hunters. We're hunting people. We hunt. You don't sell land until you have to," Randall says with conviction. Despite his physical limitations, he obviously sees himself one with the land for a long time to come. His father hunted until he was 88 and lived to be 99. "I am a mountain man," says Randall with a self-satisfied and reflective shake of the head, and quotes a poem he wrote to reinforce his statement.

"When you're born and raised that way it's part of your life. I was born to hunt." "He was born with a gun in his hands," says Gladys in a continuing counterpoint, not always adulatory. Randall's sturdy ego doesn't seem to notice.

The woods are part of Randall's fiber, not just for hunting or for lumbering. It's where he feels the best, sitting and communing with nature, and respecting it, too. He takes me along for a ride in his pickup truck to see for myself the glory of the Stover woods, still part of the original Stover 18th century land grant. A neighbor, he explains, has been given permission to clear out trees felled in a recent storm. Randall surveys his progress as we drive along. "There's no first growth left. It's mostly hemlock," he says. But they've got some hornbeam, cucumber, gumwood and ash, wild cherry, silver and red birch, red, white and black oak, black walnut, and red, hard and curly maple, he's pleased to note. "Hey, look! There's some bear claw marks up to seven feet high on that cucumber tree." He points to some long streaky tears in the bark. "Bears go crazy over that cucumber!" Personally, he hasn't seen a bear in two years although an old bear known as "Ben" is said to be in the vicinity. Randall fed Ben once. "He was just like a person. Animals and people grew up together here," he observes. Grey wolves and coyotes are known in these parts, but Randall has never seen them. He picks a pungent sprig of pennyroyal and hands it to me. "Makes a tea good for what ails you."

Randall is also a dowser of no mean accomplishment, as he and former neighbor Lawrence Wolfe will attest. He started in the 1940s and has never picked a dry hole in 300 tries. Any forked stick will

Randall Stover dowsing for graves. Photo by Michele Mott, Centre Daily Times

do. His twin brother Russell doesn't have the knack, Randall is pleased to note. But when Randall gets close to a water source, "that stick pulls down and there's no way you can hold it."

Wolfe, an energetic, handsome, white-haired, fourth generation architect, had been living on Route 45 in Millheim in a former tombstone craft shop when we met. He was born and raised a "shouting Methodist" in Pittsburgh over 80 years ago. He joined the Quakers while attending Swarthmore, but after a while had trouble with their idea of consensus and moved on. The rural life of Penns Valley is where he chose to settle. He felt himself to be an outsider but worked hard to become part of his community. When he lived on Plum Street in Aaronsburg near Randall, he learned much of the old German ways by observing the behavior of Randall and other old-time residents. He discovered silent boundaries, an innate reticence. Wives have their place and they'd better not trespass. When Wolfe first moved next door, he and his wife walked over with a bouquet of flowers as an opening gesture of neighborliness. "We don't give flowers around here," he was told, as their gift was awkwardly accepted. Nor do they shake or extend a hand in greeting. One explanation is that most of the Aaronsburgers grew up on farms in isolation and had no need for social graces. The first milking of the day was at 4 a.m. and their hands were otherwise engaged. Interaction with outsiders was minimal. They were self-sufficient. And that self-sufficiency and unfamiliarity with social graces may contribute to the fact that the town of Aaronsburg has the same population count today as it did over 200 years ago.

Hunting exploits fill Randall's mind, even those from long ago. Nowadays, the prey, or challenge, depending on one's attitude, is mainly deer and wild turkey. With relish he tells me about when, in 1856, a man named Lewis Dorman shot the last panther seen roaming these parts. After it attacked a pig in Dorman's barn he tracked it down and killed all seven feet of it, which is mighty impressive even though three and one-half feet were its tail. On his way home around dusk, Dorman stopped at his neighbor's farmhouse, tapped at the window and stuck the panther's face against the glass. It scared the bejeezuz out of young Ida Hosterman. The tawny colored panther was stuffed and eventually housed at Albright College, which returned it to Woodward for display in the celebration of its centennial during Fall Festival. Ida grew up to marry a Motz and become Randall's grandmother on his mother's side.

Although hunting season is limited in time, inveterate hunters like Randall spend many hours in the woods in preparation, long before the season starts. It's the love of the mountain that draws them. Randall is basically a tree hunter or was, until he acquired his artificial knee. But now he has to draw the line and not climb up too high. "When you're up in a tree, turkey won't see you as quick, deer won't wig you, they won't smell you, they won't see you, and yet it's natural hiding." Whether the object is deer or wild turkey, the selected tree and its surroundings have to be trimmed of interfering leaves and branches for the best line of fire. You strategize and stalk and take your time deciding. The limit is one deer or one turkey in each season and Randall doesn't hurry. He carefully chooses the perfect specimen.

Over time, some of the potential targets turn into friends. There was one old doe he used to feed out of season. "Some bastard shot her last August," he says in a quiet fury. "She was that tame. She'd eat out of my hand." Wistful now, Randall insists that when his brother showed, she wouldn't. But she knew Randall's truck and would make an appearance whenever he did. She followed him around like a dog, he tells me. One day, in a clearing, while the doe was feeding out of his hand she stopped, looked at him, turned around, made a small noise, and out of the thicket her faun came near, with his mother's assurance, for Randall to admire. "That's how close I am with wildlife," he boasts.

So there's the killing and there's the closeness. Randall has his own rules and sensibilities. The herd does have to be balanced off he rationalizes. "We love the meat. We love it." Most people say it has a wild taste. "Ours never has," chimes in Gladys when we're back in their kitchen. Randall explains that there's a whole procedure with killing venison. "Taking care of it properly is where on its anatomy you shoot it. I have never gut shot a deer in my life. Never. And when you dress it, you remove the entrails. The big thing there is, soon as you get that out is you cut the scent patches off its back legs. Then, when you get it home, you get the hide off of it just as quick as you can, when it's warm yet. And we have never, never, never had a deer that had a wild taste." Randall glows.

With wild turkeys, it's another story. The best age for hunting depends more on the feed. If they eat the insects known as walking sticks or double darning needles, they taste fishy. "But I haven't seen a double darning needle in 20 years," he admits. "If they eat acorns and they're fat, they're good. If they live basically on buds and greens and things like that, they're not so fat." He's never shot a wild turkey they couldn't eat, although some old ones have been mighty tough.

There's an art to turkey hunting, and a strategy, he informs me. Turkeys just don't come to you. They have to be called. Randall makes his own turkey callers out of slate and wood, even though they can be easily bought commercially. He prefers soft wood, usually butternut or redwood. Reaching into a nearby kitchen cupboard he pulls one out. When he blows, it makes a very realistic turkey squawking sound. "I only use this 'til I have a bird coming in that I can almost see. Then I talk with my throat—no diaphragm or anything—just with my throat." He demonstrates with what sounds to me like surprisingly accurate turkey talk.

Back in the fall of 1987 or '88, Randall was in a tree a few weeks before the fall season. While trimming branches for deer hunting, seventeen bearded toms walked right under him. "Oh, my God," he thought, "I'll never see them again." But come the first day of the season, he called them and they all came. "Seventeen bearded toms!" He shot one weighing 21½ pounds. That one had three individual beards. A beard, they say, is a growth of feathers, but it looks like stiff hair or a horsetail. The length and number of its beards can determine the age of a tom. The yearling gobbler just has a bush, the next year five inches, the next nine, the next 11, hardly ever any longer than 11 inches. The spurs on their feet start off as bumps the first year and grow longer every year. Randall has shot 46 gobblers, one for each year he's hunted.

Recently turkey-hunting rules have been changed, from one to two seasons, spring and fall. But Randall only hunts turkey in the fall. "I won't harm them in the spring when they're lovesick. It isn't fair. In spring a gobbler only has one thing on his brain. When I was young and had that on my brain, anyone could have walked up and hit me on the head!"

Randall knew of a venerable gobbler he had been trying to get for four years. The game commission warden approached him one day and asked him to shoot the bird out of season, because this tom was so unusual he should be on display. His spurs were said to be two inches long, he had 13 inches of beard and probably weighed 28 pounds. The very next morning Randall called the bird in and "could have spit in his face" within six feet. But no, he was too pretty to shoot. And by now Randall also felt they knew each other. So naturally, he had to let the bird go. When asked if he got the gobbler and Randall said he hadn't, the warden said knowingly, "I knew you wouldn't." Two years later, he found the gobbler's remains in the woods, and the spurs were two and one-half inches long. After finding other traces, Randall put them all on a pile and stood there looking at them and said, in a manner that seemed almost prayerful in the retelling, "Well, buddy, I didn't get you. But here's where you belong."

And here, in Penns Valley, is where Randall belongs. He is at home and is part of its rhythm. Unlike his forebears who hunted for all their food, and fought the enemy, he carries on the tradition but obeys the current laws. He takes his quota of one deer and one turkey a season, and knows how to prepare them. He gleans from his surroundings. He fishes and scours for berries. He dowses for springs, and remarkably, more recently for lost graves in old cemeteries, a little known practice but one Randall swears by. He whittles the wood from his hills. He supports his church and his civic association and speaks up for the preservation of his way of life.

The Miner

Middle-aged, middle-sized, slightly paunchy Irvin "Les" Confer is facing a standoff, loins girded, his resources and heavy political clout butted nose to nose against people of Penns Valley, who are in some cases united against what they see as his onslaught to their quality of life. Confer wants to get on with the job, he tells me, of strip mining for top grade Valentine limestone concentrated in a large near-the-surface seam of 96 to 98 percent pure calcium carbonate that runs south of Aaronsburg,

We are at Confer's combined home and office in Milesburg, off a four-lane highway, adjacent to a sprawling trailer park. At the time of our visit he and his family have lived here for the last 20 years and it's not your typical suburban neighborhood. Leading me down to his basement office, he points out framed photographs of a Little League team his company sponsors. Once seated at his desk he tells me that Confers, who today fill an entire page in the Centre County telephone book, have always worked the land in these parts, in one way or another, in the 1700s and 1800s by farming and timbering, and in this century by mining for hard coal first, and now Valentine limestone.

Two brothers of the German-Dutch Confer family settled nearby in the late 1700s, about nine miles from where Les now lives. One brother settled up on the north branch of the Susquehanna, and he or his descendants changed the spelling to Confair. Les mentions with pride that Interstate 80 is known as the Confare Highway, but when questioned about the exact origins or location of the family in Germany he cannot answer. Records show an Adam Confer in 1802 as one of the first settlers of Millheim, and a John Confer who appeared as witness at a murder trial in 1818.

His enterprises, says Les, are what the economy of Centre County was founded on, and needs today in order to survive. As Barbara Brueggebors, former reporter of the *Centre Daily Times* puts it, "Limestone is literally the bedrock of Centre County. The valleys rest on it. So does a very basic part of the economy and infrastructure." And the product, Confer claims, is essential for use as agricultural lime in water purification, in making toothpaste, in degreasing and in glassmaking. A 75-foot solid seam of Valentine limestone exists throughout the area, sometimes parallel to the ground, sometimes perpendicular or at a descending angle, based on the movement and buckling of the earth millions of years ago. At that time the area was an ocean floor built up by the bones and shells of sea creatures. Confer's company, Con-Stone, Inc., has been mining the Bellefonte ledge underground about 30 miles northwest of Aaronsburg near his home, where the ledge runs vertical and deep. They're bringing up 96 to 99 percent pure calcium carbonate stone at the rate of 2,000 tons a day, 23 tons per load, taking 80 to 90 truckloads a day.

Just outside the town lines of Aaronsburg, in Haines Township, on a hill about 2,000 feet above town, parallel to Route 45 to be precise, Confer has started operations on a surface mine. He owns a little less than 500 acres of farmland, which he bought for $1.1 million from Centre Foods, which, in turn, bought a total of 2,700 acres of farmland from the Bethlehem Steel Company in 1988. And he bought it at farm acreage, not mine site, which sells at a higher price. Quite a bargain.

Bethlehem Steel slowly amassed farmland in Penns Valley near Aaronsburg from the 1920s until foreign competition and obsolescence of facilities caused the shrinking of the steel industry starting in the 1950s.

Planning ahead, the steel company held on to the land to have a readily available source of Valentine limestone, whenever they might need it for the old blast furnace smelting process for ironmaking. In most cases the farms were then rented to their former owners. In the intervening 70 years the tenant farmers lived on and worked the Bethlehem land, locally known as "steel farms."

When Bethlehem switched from the open hearth to the basic oxygen furnace in the 1960s, the company no longer had as much need for limestone. The land had lost its primary use for the company. As long as it was beneficial from a tax standpoint, the company maintained the 21 farms. But once the land was sold to another mining company, the same ominous cloud covering Naginey's limestone mine soon would be threatening the quality of life of the residents of Penns Valley.

Casual observers driving by over the years got the false impression, as did I, that industry had somehow bypassed the whole ridge valley region, leaving its appearance pretty much the way it was for the last two centuries. We saw rolling farmland ribboned with undulating strips of contoured fields, subdued brown stubble in fall and winter, expectant golds and greens in spring and summer. Little did we realize the disruption that lay ahead and below.

Twice, this tiny village has been awakened from its 18th century Brigadoon-like reverie, both times by the coming of outsiders. The first time, in 1949, was with the "Aaronsburg Story" pageant. In the second awakening in the 1990s, some townspeople of Aaronsburg were mobilized once again to a smaller extent, responding now to the threat of invasion by the Confer forces' mining assault on their tranquil countryside. And, as before, the incursion has drawn reaction in widening circles, spreading far beyond this sleepy village. This time the interested parties were historians, archaeologists, geologists, environmentalists, trout fishermen, cavers and citizens concerned, in general, with the quality of life in the Valley. The Penns Valley Conservation Association, composed of all of the above, and especially mobilized to tackle this problem, has been waging an aggressive campaign to block or limit the operation of the mine. Could they be seen in some quarters as invaders, too?

Hosterman's Pit, considered by cavers to be the largest and richest in cave artifacts in Centre County, and the best sporting cave in all of Pennsylvania, lies on top of the Valentine vein on the Confer mine site. It is a solution cave, meaning that its limestone started breaking down millions of years ago, forming many sinkholes and the myriad caves all along Route 45. Hosterman's Pit will not survive the mining operations. Valentine limestone does not dissolve readily but forms a dense layer, unlike the surrounding limestone.

In the early 1960s, the Nittany Grotto, a local cavers' association in nearby State College, entered into a formal agreement with Bethlehem Steel to manage Hosterman's Pit, limiting access to experienced cavers only. The entrance to the cave was small and the immediate descent steep and maneuverable only by experts. Since taking over, Confer has cut off the cavers' access to it and to nearby Stover's cave as well. He literally welded shut the opening, as he says, "to show ownership."

The cavers were naturally distressed to have lost access to the cave for their exploration and sport. Until they were barred, they had investigated over 6,000 feet of passages covering 17 acres, finding stalactites and stalagmites, columns and flowstone. "Shipsprow room," "Feick's frustration," and "Nevin's heaven" are a few of their pet names for these unusual spaces. Archaeologists, geologists, and biologists, too, from The Carnegie Museum of Natural History in Pittsburgh and elsewhere, pleaded for an opportunity to examine and preserve specimens of fauna dating back to the end of the Ice Age, over 9,000 years ago. Before sealing the cave entrance, Confer gave the Pennsylvania Historical and Museum Commission only one day's grace to collect and remove their artifacts and bones. He required them to sign a confidentiality agreement to the effect that they wouldn't tell what relics of value were found until all appeals were exhausted.

Many Aaronsburg residents envisioned the havoc that a major mining project would create on the entire area, which is solely residential and farmland. Underground, it would affect aquifers and wells and subvert, they feared, the quality of their drinking water. Aboveground, air quality would be threatened by the drilling and pervasive blasted stone dust to be crushed on site. The noise from blasting would violate the rural stillness, upsetting to both people and cattle. And their main thoroughfare, Route 45, a two-lane road only lightly used today, would be invaded by the non-stop heavy traffic and noise and vibration of the passage of 50 limestone-laden trucks every day. Lightweight Amish buggies and their skittish horses could easily be edged off the berm into ditches.

Under his peaked cap, this is how Les Confer sees his people problem: some old-timers would rather have a quarry than a housing development, most Amish are neutral, and the new people are dead set against him. Bruce Teeple, the local museum director, is a relatively recent arrival, but a dedicated Aaronsburger. He notes ironically that the Valentine limestone Confer seeks is so pure it will be used for smokestack filter material. And, in the course of extracting it, the mining process will pollute the entire area around Aaronsburg in order to improve other people's environment elsewhere.

"I can understand those people's concern," Les tells me, "but it's something that's needed and it's there and that's what our corporation does. That's just the way of life and just another step towards progress, I guess." He's right that the old-timers have grown up since the twenties with the notion that Bethlehem Steel was planning one day to mine the area. Many of them, like the Musicks, were steel farm tenants themselves, so they are more accepting of what to them, is the inevitable. Ardranna Musick says Centre Foods, which ran a local cannery, tried to farm for vegetables. But it was a dry summer and so they sold the land to Confer. Today the Musicks quietly accept the invasion of a limestone-mining project. Sure, Ralph and Ardranna have nice memories of old Aaronsburg. "Whadya gonna do?" asks Musick. "It's progress." On the other hand, the newcomers, having left pollution behind in their large cities, appreciate the rarity of the valley's pure air, water and quietude and are willing to fight to preserve it. Many of them were unaware of Bethlehem Steel's history in Centre County and feel betrayed.

In its campaign against the mining project, the Penns Valley Conservation Association claimed the quarry would have a negative impact on the entire area, well beyond Aaronsburg itself. Fishermen from the Trout, Unlimited organization, who represent another important local industry—tourism and recreation—predicted the warming and befouling of nearby "exceptional value" trout streams as a consequence of mining an area known for its porous substructure and many sinkholes. They proved, through the use of dye tests in the sinkhole Confer planned to use for mine water drainage, that the subterranean waters would leach into neighboring streams. Nearby Elk and Pine Creeks, widely noted for their pure water, would undoubtedly be polluted by the waste influx. As a result the creeks' temperature would be raised significantly, endangering the existence of the abundant brown trout that act as a lure for out-of-town and local fisherman. The two creeks' current ratings of "exceptional value" would be lost.

Spruce Creek, farther west off Route 45, and not involved in the current controversy, supports exclusive fishing clubs which have been hosts to a few presidents, including Dwight D. Eisenhower and Jimmy Carter. Tackle shops and fishing guides advertise in the local papers. Trout fishing in Centre County has a definite widespread mystique. To Edwin L. Peterson, writing of the glories of Pennsylvania in *Penns Woods West* in 1959, trout streams were the essence of Centre County. "Conservation does not stop . . . with making the world safe for brown trout . . . It goes far beyond that. It is a belief in a way of life, of community life, in which we can all live happily." How can we all live happily today when rural environment is being threatened by rural/industrial blight?

Randall Stover, unlike Burt Stover, is part of the anti-quarry faction, although he isn't sure of the answer. While doing renovations and repairs on one of the steel farms for Bethlehem Steel in Aaronsburg back in February 1959, Randall was hauling rock with a farm tractor. At one point, when he dug out a scoopful of rock, the front wheel of the tractor dropped down into a declivity. Randall backed off and decided to take a look, thinking he had stumbled on a groundhog hole. Detaching the side view mirror from his truck he maneuvered it, catching and angling the sunlight down the hole. He could see that the light tapered like a cone for about six feet and then dropped off suddenly. On further investigation, the hole proved to be over 100 feet deep. Randall, it turns out, was the first man to locate Hosterman's Pit. In fact, when the mining project started, he told Confer in no uncertain terms, that the mining company's plan to prevent polluting the nearby fishing streams wouldn't work. Randall knows the water tables, the local streams, how they interconnect, and the ideal temperature needed to maintain healthy brown trout.

Randall accidentally ran into Confer one day on the mine site. It had been a long time favorite spot of his for picking wild raspberries. And now he was caught trespassing. When he told Confer he was the first person to look down Hosterman's Pit, Confer countered, "Why didn't you fill it right back up?" They talked for over an hour, Randall tells me. "I know he thought I was a dumb Dutchman." "I suppose you signed that petition against me," Confer demanded. Randall said he did, unflinchingly. "If you take my pure water away, I'm goin' to be mad as hell!" "Oh, we won't interfere with that water," rejoined Confer, confidently. To me Confer had said, "mine water was no more than rain water."

Randall then told Confer how, during the forties, he had worked at Naginey, near Milroy, another Bethlehem Steel limestone quarry for more than 11 years, until it closed down. "I run the pumps then," he told Confer. When the water was discharged into Honeybrook Creek, Randall saw the creek deteriorate from a number one trout stream to nothing in five years time. The same thing, he was certain, would happen to Elk and Pine Creeks that converge in Coburn to join Penns Creek, a few miles south of the quarry site. Penns Creek winds its way to the Susquehanna River, to Chesapeake Bay, and eventually to the Atlantic Ocean.

Confer tried to reassure Randall by saying they were planning to do a dye test determining the underground water flow. As I mentioned earlier, Randall said he knew already where it would come out. He knew precisely. "Above the third bridge below Millheim on Elk Creek," he predicted. "And the rest over on Pine." After the test, Randall's conclusion proved to be right on target. He knows his territory, from way underground, up. Randall also happens to be a dowser. "Now over at Milroy all they have is a big hole with water. And that's what we'll have here," Randall tells me, with a disheartened and resigned shrug. "A big hole. Not to mention shattered windows and sickness from diesel fumes. You can't beat big money," Randall sighs.

Helen Fahy, is a slim, dark-eyed, intense young woman, who was the first president of the Penns Valley Conservation Association. She is not a native of the valley, as is the case with many of the group's members. With a few exceptions, old-timers who are members are not active except when there's a special event. Helen came from Detroit to Penn State for a degree in Environmental Engineering, specializing in water. She and her husband, Joe, loved the lush green of the valley and decided to settle in after graduation. No more up at dawn to beat urban commuter traffic, they hoped. So 20 years ago they bought the 1846 former log tollhouse, located on Route 45 near Spring Mills, and slowly worked at improving it. Here, in Penns Valley, the Fahys were amazed to find no one locks their doors. They had found a community of friends who appreciate the unpressured rhythm of life. Many, like themselves, could live anywhere. The Fahy's clients of their Water Quality Management

Consultants, Inc., come from all over the state. But the prospect of the continued pollution of their Eden had them all up in arms. Leaning against their barn right on Route 45, a rough hand painted sign read: "SAVE PENNS 'CRIK.' STOP THE CON-STONE QUARRY!"

After graduation from Penn State, Helen worked for the Pennsylvania Department of Environmental Resources (DER), now called the Department of Environmental Protection (DEP). In 1992, it was she who reviewed Confer's permit application for the mine and realized that long ago Elk and Pine Creeks had been misclassified. For years they were on a list for upgrading to "exceptional value," a designation of the highest purity of water. In the back of her mind was the memory of the harrowing sight of the River Rouge in her hometown of Detroit, actually on fire from pollution. This spurred her on to clinch the long overdue upgrade.

Confer started preparing the site in early 1997, and extracting Valentine limestone later in the year, despite appeals to the Pennsylvania Department of Environmental Protection and a lawsuit brought by the coalition. As the result of a prickly settlement prior to trial some important restrictions have been placed by DEP on Con-Stone's *modus operandi*. Due to the "exceptional value" classification, Confer may not mine beyond 1,080 feet below sea level, nor may he pump water. In addition, the company has had to install aboveground water filtering systems, rather than fill the existing sinkholes with treated water, which would eventually find its way to the trout streams. Con-Stone had not yet installed needed pollution sedimentation control measures. However, through some perverse, but not uncommon reckoning, it is up to the opponents to prove damage to the environment, not the State agency.

Originally, the Penns Valley Conservation Association, rather than the State agency, was responsible for monitoring the streams to ascertain the water quality. They installed a "turbidity meter" in Pine Creek to take continuous readings of TSS (total suspended solids) every half hour. DEP has taken charge of the coalition's meter, installed a second one, yet holds PVCA liable for any repairs. The allies have hired a biologist from Penn State to sample the activities of fish. But expenses borne solely by the coalition limit surveillance time. Potluck dinners, the annual fundraising PVCA house tour, plus solicitation of funds from members and friends, keep them limping along financially. Support for their cause comes from throughout Penns Valley all the way from Woodward to Boalsburg, with members opening their homes and giving of their time.

A wide swath of grey limestone road slices through the field and tree line where Randall Stover once sought his wild raspberries. As a result of the opponents' insistence, mining activities have been set back quite far from the main road. The mine area is completely off-limits to outsiders. However, what I saw, as a Sunday trespasser who ignored the "Blasting area warning signal" signs, and drove up to the mine site when no guards were around, was idle elephantine-sized equipment, crushers, derricks and high piles of slag reminiscent of the pyramids at Ghiza.

Although there is an increase in truck traffic along Route 45, as of now the mine is apparently not fully operational. Con-Stone has put high piles of landfill at the borders abutting other people's property as sound buffers. Nevertheless some neighbors have installed seismographs to register the vibrations from detonations of blasting material.

At present, there's a standoff. Ominous predictions of a ruined valley have not been realized. But as yet the mining operations are in low gear. Test results of water pollution are not in. What will be the role of the State Department of Environmental Protection? Will they actually protect the environment? The members of the Penns Valley Conservation Association, 40 years after Edwin Peterson's comments, are facing a common dilemma and it's still not just how to keep the world safe for brown trout. It is about Ralph Musick's so-called progress. Are the solutions "either-or," or can seemingly conflicting needs be balanced? Early 20th century robber barons, who, after making their fortunes transformed themselves into philanthropists, gave no thought to the havoc they were imposing on the environment. Unchecked air pollution and unsafe working conditions were the norm. Today government intervention through enforced safety regulations has put a limit on these abuses, as evidenced by the restrictions imposed on the Con-Stone operations. Still, Randall Stover will have to find a new source for wild raspberries, and fortunately there are still places in Penns Valley to find them.

Chapter 9

NEW SETTLERS

The Teeples

Bruce Teeple has a strong sense of his roots. He can trace his family back over 200 years in Canada to a Hessian mercenary in the Indian wars. "We were Tories and were kicked out of here then. Matter of fact, we were kicked out of wherever we went for the last 500 years!" he says with a sardonic grin. We are sitting at his crowded table downstairs in the museum in Aaronsburg during one of many visits. His name, he tells me, comes from a Northern German dialect word for devil—*deibel*.

"I kind of get ribbed about not being a local." But Bruce happened on some old records not too long ago that were for him a thrilling revelation. It seems there was a group of men known as Robinson's Rangers just before the Revolutionary War, who banded together for protection against Indian attacks. Since the militia had disbanded, these self-styled rangers patrolled the area from the west branch of the Susquehanna down to Penns Creek. And there on the roster were three Teeples! "Robinson's Rangers, pre-Revolution! Can you beat that? I sure queered that with the Stovers!" His roots in Penns Valley are deeper than he imagined.

I wonder why people pursue genealogy. Teeple has found an interesting pattern in those who come to his museum searching for their roots. Those of German descent have no illusions. Their ancestors were either farmers or tradesmen or a Hessian mercenary, such as those Bruce traces his ancestry to. Those of English descent "desperately want to find a branch of their family tree linked, however illegitimately, to British royalty. Whatever the reason," he assures me, "we take solace and seek meaning in, and we draw sustenance from discovering our rootedness in time and place." While helping others uncover their roots, he has developed an approach toward work as he does with everything in life, "whether it's mixing concrete, digging ditches or working in the museum ... because it's fun!" When work is seen as something to avoid, "it no longer becomes a true part of our deepest selves."

Although he's a relative newcomer to the area, Bruce has worked conscientiously to become part of his adopted community of Aaronsburg. In addition to the many hours he devotes to the museum, he serves as secretary of the local water company. His wife, Michelle, a teacher and librarian, is on the board of the Aaronsburg Library and a diligent volunteer for the Dutch Fall Festival. Her family has deep roots in Pennsylvania, too, as early English and Dutch settlers.

During their years as undergraduates at Penn State, Bruce and Michelle drove between their homes near Philadelphia in the Schuylkill Valley, back and forth on Route 45 through Buffalo and Penns Valleys. They fell in love with the rich rolling farmland, and determined that here was where they eventually wanted to live. Bruce earned a bachelor's degree in history and political science. They both planned to teach. But he was passed over for service during the Vietnam War due to a grade school basketball injury that left him with two screws in his arm. Without the cushion of benefits from the G. I. education bill, despite working and studying part-time, Bruce never got his teaching certification. Determined to stay in Penns Valley, he wound up working full time in the maintenance department at Penn State.

E. F. Schumacher, in *Small is Beautiful*, says "There are people in search of a new life style, who seek to return to certain basic truths about man and his world. I call them home-comers." Bruce and Michelle Teeple are home-comers. At first they rented an old farmhouse in Woodward that they had eyed wistfully from Route 45 during their undergraduate peregrinations. They soon adapted to the rigors of farm life and fell into an easy relationship with their Amish neighbors. Bruce, who definitely speaks his mind, was their defender against picture-taking tourists who insensitively snapped at the "quaint" costumes and "charming" buggies. As John Hostetler confirms in *Amish Society*, "to take or pose for pictures is specifically forbidden in Amish law." Beyond the Old Testament prohibition of the graven image (Exodus 20:4-5), Bruce explains that if you define yourself as part of a community, as the Amish do, by allowing your picture to be taken you have set yourself above the group. Eventually, after the birth of Jane, their second daughter, the isolation of their remote location and need for the security and support of closer neighbors that a village would provide convinced the Teeples to leave the farm. And so the move to East Plum Street in Aaronsburg.

Ronald Blythe, in *Akenfield: Portrait of an English Village*, puts it this way: "The first thing a newcomer does when arriving in a village is to begin to claim it . . . he simply starts to feel his way towards the village identity, recognize it for what it is and shape himself to fit it. He will often envy the old indigenous stock . . . but in effect his life will be freer than theirs. The sometimes crushing, limiting power which the village exerts on families which have never escaped will be unknown to him." The Teeples have come to recognize the "limiting power" and work around it.

It is Bruce and Michelle's attitude toward honest labor that has eased the Teeples' absorption into the life style and rhythm and pace of the original settlers, and serves as a common thread with the newly arrived Amish into small town life. *Arbeit* is Bruce's operative word. "Work is a great leveler," he tells me, while balancing his large frame on the two back legs of a kitchen chair. We have just come into their house after surveying his half-acre vegetable garden. Michelle is busy preparing dinner in their kitchen-family room that takes up the whole width of the back of their ground floor. "It's that common thread I find, the thing I have in common with the Amish," he tells me. "They respect me and the Germans around here in the valley. They respect a person that's a worker whether you're working for the community, your family or your job."

I ask him what kind of caps he and Michelle have kept on their lives. "If you have a choice of sitting on your ass and watching TV on a summer's night or working in the garden—you work in the garden! I tell my kids, bedrooms are for two things—and one of them is sleeping. Don't spend your life in your room. Get outside and do something!" When first I heard him say *Arbeit*, the image I couldn't help project was the *Arbeit macht freiheit* hung ironically over the entrance to the concentration camp at Dachau. But "Work makes freedom" in Penns Valley has been the freed man's *modus vivendi*. "I lift cement all day," he sighs philosophically, speaking of his job in the maintenance department at Penn State.

Bruce is steeped in what he calls an agricultural ethic, which still exists in Penns Valley but he fears is slowly eroding. A respect for honest labor is one of this ethic's five distinct characteristics. Faith in the future is the second tenet. He describes how this once took form in three basic activities: saving seed; acting as a temporary steward of the land; and bringing children into the world. The Teeples subscribe to all three today. "As markets grew more complex and remote, people began interpreting this faith in the future as financial security. Their investments became less tangible. Paper symbols—be they money or stocks—replaced land, seed and children."

A third aspect of the agricultural ethic is the realization that "life is a series of interconnected, inevitable and ever-changing cycles." Stories of birth, growth, decay and rebirth always have, and always will emerge, merge and dissolve in our universal myth. All of life's events, when viewed in terms of the long run, the big picture, become much more comprehensible and interesting. City folk see a rhythm in changing seasons, but being removed from the soil we are denied the miracle of witnessing the seed sprout or the calf whelped; mine is an urban ethic.

The fourth value in Teeple's agricultural ethic is religion. "I'm not speaking here of garden variety, Sunday-go-to-meeting religion. Religion in human life was originally an integral expression of our forebears' lives." It involved accepting two fundamental ideas: that some events are just beyond our control and understanding; and that life everlasting comes from remembrance by our descendants. He gives me an illustration. "For ten years we shared a farm outside Woodward with several Amish families. Every spring Michelle and I would hear these wailing chants in the wind, as our neighbors plowed their fields. We've heard these same songs jazzed up at their wedding receptions, when the hard cider was flowing. These songs date from the time of their ancestors' persecution, when the Amishman's sense of one-ness, of community was solidified. They are the only songs the Amish know, the remnants of an oral tradition reverberating through every fiber of their being."

The fifth value of this agricultural ethic, he tells me, can best be summarized by the following story. "I once asked a woman in town how her family survived during the Depression. 'Well, I'll tell you,' she said. 'First of all, only the rich were living any differently than before. My father left my mother, my two sisters and me when I was seven years old. I only saw him one other time, when I was 12, for about ten minutes. Our biggest problem could have been heat and fuel. And yet, one fellow every year would go up in the mountain and dump several wagonloads of wood in our yard. We had to cut it and split it ourselves. No words or money were ever exchanged. Everyone around here pitched in like that. Good neighbors. That's how we survived.'" I'm interested to note how they've reconciled their sense of independence with a willingness to accept help under certain circumstances.

Aaronsburg represents stability to the Teeples. They have sunk their roots into a Levy lot house on Plum Street, down the block from the Museum and the Randall and Billy Stovers. "Everyone knows your business and nobody locks their doors," says Bruce, speaking with pride of his community. Michelle and the girls share his enthusiasm for the museum and local history. Frequently, when I've dropped by for a Saturday visit, Alice has been laboring alongside her father with new displays. "Our ancestors did not live in a vacuum. They shared many of the same concerns, choices and conflicts we have today. They had a rich, earthy sense of humor, but they were not full of themselves. It is a measure of our bonds to a soulless technological society if we are merely content with collecting names, dates or antiques, or in sacrificing neighborliness on the altar of local history. To understand ourselves, our values and our customs, we must know what came before. We are the harvest of our collective pasts. What seeds can we save for the future?"

The Teeples are also serious about their actual vegetable garden. I watch as Bruce hauls wheelbarrow loads of compost to enrich the soil. They experiment with unusual varieties of vegetables, like Rainbow Inca corn, an early open-pollinated variety to be eaten raw or cooked. Bruce favors Polish tomatoes, big, blocky with lots of meat. Michelle does the canning.

At season's end, their back porch floor is blotched and stained with leaky, rotting tomatoes whose seeds they will save for next year's planting. They do not stray too far from home, save for an occasional family excursion to an historical site like Gettysburg. So far they have not accepted my invitation to visit Pittsburgh. I have not had to ask them why. But Bruce and Michelle are in tune with the pulse of their lives in Aaronsburg, in rhythm with their roots, old and new.

The Sarnows

As a child, growing up near Lake Champlain in the Adirondack Mountains of upper New York State, Eric Sarnow was a picky eater. His steady diet consisted of peanut butter for lunch and lamb chops and steak for dinner. Like many kids, he never touched vegetables. A few years ago, as chef of his own restaurant, peanut butter was still on hand in the kitchen of the original Hummingbird Room Inn in Woodward. Dreaming of samples of gourmet cuisine when I came for our first interview at noon on a day the restaurant was closed, I learned this to my chagrin. The owner and chef of the finest restaurant along the 100 mile length of Route 45 offered me a peanut butter sandwich on white, pleasantly with no apologies, at half past two when it seemed likely that we needed a lot more time to talk. After I wolf down the sandwich he does offer to poach a chicken breast, but I demur resolutely. This says a lot for Eric's independent, confident and relaxed attitude in the first restaurant he ever ran on his own. And it was located in an isolated tiny town of 250 inhabitants at the eastern end of Penns Valley, 25 miles in either direction from his principal sources of patronage, State College and Lewisburg.

Eric and his wife, Claudia, opened the Hummingbird Room in November 1993. The Sarnows were the most recent settlers in the town of Woodward. They started their restaurant on a shoestring, carting used kitchen equipment and paraphernalia gradually in

many trips from Philadelphia to the Woodward Inn, whose history dated back to the first settlers, the Motzes, who built it in 1814. The Hosterman family bought the Inn from the Motz family in the 1860s, and some member of that family had been running it ever since. In an area noted for its hunting and trout fishing, close to woodland hiking and skiing

Eric Sarnow sautéing zucchini flowers. Photo *by Pat Little,* Centre Daily Times.

trails, near Woodward Cave, the inn had drawn tourists in all seasons throughout the year, as it drew travelers on horseback in the 1800s. Cloyd Steininger from Lewisburg who "spent time recovering from a nervous breakdown" wrote these timeless lines in 1945 in the Inn's guest book:

"In finding this we found the best.

In Centre County at Woodward Inn—
This the place we have been,
We came for much needed rest,
A large stone house of native stone
Built in Eighteen and Fourteen,
At center point in old Penn State,
In a luscious spot on a great highway—
This road a turnpike used to be—
Now it's "Highway-Lakes-to-Sea."

(To the memory of my departed friend and former proprietor of Woodward Inn, Wesley S. Hosterman and the residents of Woodward, these lines are most affectionately dedicated.)

Back then the restaurant served typical Pennsylvania Dutch food, with shoo fly pie and apple pan dowdy, balancing seven sweets with seven sours, perhaps an inspiration for our poet. The current owner, Chris Hosterman Doren and her husband, John, came back from Minnesota in 1986 to continue the family tradition when her mother retired. Since their career interests lay in education and computer software design, not innkeeping, they eventually sought alternate means to keep the old traditional inn going. They found a brilliant solution in the Sarnows, to whom they offered the opportunity to reopen the restaurant.

To Eric, Woodward reminded him of his Adirondack home with its proximity to woods and fishing. Claudia knew and was comfortable with the area. Her best friend lived in Mifflinburg 15 miles east over the Narrows in neighboring Buffalo Valley. Like Bruce and Michelle Teeple, Claudia had attended Penn State. She worked in State College restaurants where she specialized in baking and pastry. She was an artist looking for a profession, and here in Woodward, as pastry chef, hostess and designer of menus, Claudia Sarnow could fulfill her creative urges in a practical manner. Eric, who should know, considers her a natural baker. "She has great taste buds. Her desserts are works of art."

Eric prides himself on his sauces. His secret? "Reduction, reduction, reduction." He had a solid 13 years of culinary training, three of them in France as apprentice to chefs at Chateau d'Artigny and the Relais Chateau at Montbazon. Since his mother is French, Eric has dual nationality and was able to work abroad as a Frenchman. His maternal grandfather ran a restaurant in Deauville. At the Domaine de Beauvois, Eric's title was *chef de parti*, which was a position under the *sous-chef*. Before opening the Hummingbird Room, Eric had the rank of *sous-chef*, second in command, under chef Georges Perrier at Le Bec Fin, the finest restaurant in Philadelphia.

Claudia, a tall imposing woman with dark hair, vivid blue eyes and magnificent carriage, was expecting their first child. They anguished over Eric's long hours, working from 10 a.m. to 1 a.m. at Le Bec Fin. What would that mean to the quality of life they sought as a young expanding family? It was scary to think of their child eventually having to go through metal detectors at the Philadelphia public schools. Is this where they wanted to live? Claudia remembered during her years at Penn State that there were other outsiders, "hippies," students, some dropout city kids, who settled nearby in Coburn, and found Penns Valley a healthy place to live.

Within one month, in May 1993, fate took charge and ordained a change. Their son, Evan, was born prematurely, weighing only one and one-half pounds. At the same time Eric's beloved father died. "So much trauma," Eric recalls, "after that, what was the worst thing that could happen?" He remembered his father's wise words, "When you make a decision for the rest of your life, make sure it's doing something you really like." Evan, they say, made the decision for them. It was a leap of faith, starting a new life. By the end of July, Evan weighed four and one-half pounds, and the three Sarnows were on their way to Penns Valley.

They moved to Woodward in August. Eric and Claudia set themselves a goal of three months time to refurbish the kitchen and dining rooms, recycling everything usable the Dorens provided. Just at this awkward moment, Eric snapped his Achilles tendon, and his leg had to be immobilized in a cast. His accident, so close to the opening, left all of the painting to Claudia. Ever inventive, after stripping off old wallpaper she redid the dining room walls using Evan's diapers in a texturing technique she called "raggy diapering," producing an interesting mottled effect. The kitchen and menu design were her responsibility as well, and she dug in with relish.

Realistically eyeing their purse, as they held high their goal of serving the highest quality food, Eric and Claudia did not even consider the Bec Fin four-star level of elegance, which demanded the use of crystal, porcelain and silver. Instead, they were satisfied with chairs and tables of individual character and size and serviceable china and cutlery. Once the freshly pressed maroon cloths and napkins were on, the lights dimmed and candles lit, the effect would do quite nicely.

Concerted effort went into locating nearby suppliers of fresh produce and meat, and finding local help. Miraculously they appeared. During my visit, teenager Jenny Arndt stopped by and timidly offered samples of lettuces from her garden, butter crunch and curly endive. Another neighbor planted unusual lettuces, frizé and radicchio. An Amish farmer, Stephen Esh, delivered zucchini blossoms. Lance Mellon, a neighbor in Woodward and originally from Pittsburgh, developed a rewarding way of life for himself growing and selling produce on his farm to area restaurants. He was another supplier.

The Sarnows started planting their own herbs and edible flowers. Eric found an excellent source in nearby Spring Mills at Meyers Meats, an immaculate fourth generation butcher shop, which is open only on the weekends, a practice Eric decided to follow at his restaurant. The Hummingbird Room opened on time in November to serve dinner on Friday, Saturday and Sunday from five to nine. With the chef still hobbling around in his cast, they offered a gourmet French menu undreamed of in the 200 year history of the Woodward Inn. And the people came.

Hummingbird Room. Photo by Joan Morse Gordon.

The people came to such an extent that five years later, the Sarnows were able to buy a beautiful old brick Gothic Revival house in Spring Mills, 12 miles west of Woodward. A tasteful Hummingbird Room sign hangs from the white gingerbread porch. Right on Route 45, closer to the populous State College, the house sits amidst giant weeping willow trees on a broad lawn that sweeps down to a stream where the neighbor's Holsteins refresh themselves. Known as *Auchentorlie*, the house was built in 1847. Major Jared P. Fisher, who was a direct descendant of Palatine settlers, bought the property in 1881 and apparently spared no expense on its improvement. He installed the first flush toilet in Centre County, which now is located, though not in use, at the museum in Aaronsburg. During the conversion from private home to restaurant, the Sarnows kept finding relics of the past: the original front door key, a Civil War belt buckle, and old photographs.

The new Hummingbird Room has achieved the level of elegance the Sarnows put in abeyance in Woodward, in order to create and maintain the high level of cuisine they prized above all. Everything here is grander; the decor is more elegant; the kitchen is bigger and has better equipment; the dining room has a larger capacity; the staff has grown, as has Evan. The Sarnows still count on local people for everything, from construction to staff, to fresh produce.

Like Michelle and Bruce Teeple, Claudia and Eric and Evan are living where they want to be, doing what they want to do most, just as his father advised. All they need, they have found in Penns Valley.

Chapter 10

OVER THE HILL & BACK

Bill Heim and the Scarlet D

At one time there were six hotels in Mifflinburg. Now there's only one. The Mifflinburg Hotel, which houses the Scarlet D restaurant is a three-story Federal style building built as the Deckard Hotel in 1858 on the site of the earlier Stitz. Around 1916, it was known as the Hopp Hotel. At that time it acquired a three-tier wraparound porch. On the path of the original Lewisburg-Mifflinburg Turnpike, the site has undoubtedly been used as an inn and tavern since the late 1790s. It probably served as a stop on the first stagecoach route from Northumberland through Aaronsburg to Bellefonte.

The original hotel burned down in 1818. The tavern's name, the Scarlet D, derives from an old custom when beer was sold by the pint or quart, and regular customers' names were listed on a board and marked after each purchase, forcing them to mind their "P's" and "Q's." Those who overindulged were required to wear a placard painted with a scarlet "D" for drunkard to announce to the unsuspecting their state of intemperance.

Earlier, the hotel was run by Adam and George Wilt, the sons of miller George Wilt who came up north from Cumberland County and settled in the Narrows. From 1810 to 1818, Adam Wilt and a partner,

John Fisher, used an alternative form of transportation, water. They ran arks, which were little more than flat-bottomed wooden boxes water-proofed with packed tar and pitch on a planked raft, 50 by 13 feet. These were filled with raw timber, grain or whiskey, linseed oil and other finished products from farms in the valley and floated down Penns Creek into the Susquehanna River, which empties eventually into Chesapeake Bay at Havre de Grace, Maryland. Adam Wilt is remembered as the first man to run the treacherous Conewago Falls, south of Harrisburg, with an ark.

Running arks was a one-way operation, and only during high water in early spring, when melting snows and heavy rains raised the water level. At other times both the creek and the river were and still are shallow and rocky and treacherous. Picture the raftsmen, a pilot, a steersman and a bowsman, poling along in their coonskin caps and frock coats, stroking and singing in time to the fiddler on deck as they passed the sawmills and villages long since gone. Once the arks arrived downstream as far as Havre de Grace, they would be dismantled, the wood recycled at its destination, leaving the navigators to find other means of transportation back. Usually the raftsmen returned by foot through woods, where they might encounter panthers or wolves on their way home.

When Bill Heim took over the Mifflinburg Hotel in 1978 it had been a rooming house for some time and needed a lot of refurbishing.

John Libby, pasty-pale, soft, round, bent and bewhis-kered, was a tenant then, and still has his room today after 27 years. Bill's wife, Chris, shrugs, accepting the fact that John came with the building. Refurbishing had to be done around him. John grew up in Penns Creek and worked at a cabinet

Mifflinburg Hotel and The Scarlet D Restaurant. Photo by Joan Morse Gordon.

factory in Mifflinburg. His bulky, Zero Mostel-like frame shuffles downstairs at mealtime, spends the evening in his room and sits quietly for a short time in the lobby with his iced tea and a bowl of chips before bedtime. Sometimes he talks to people who work there. Weekly guests take care of their own rooms. Chris says John's looks terrible.

Starting from scratch, Bill fixed the place up in a Victorian mode with old things he picked up here and there. He relied on the experienced eye he developed when he owned the Back Door antique shop in Lewisburg. Bill believes in recycling. The front desk enclosure with its new stained glass window was the teller booth from the Lewisburg National Bank. Two long polished dark wood bars with gleaming brass bar rails and beer taps and the heavy bronze deeply embossed National cash register all help to create a warm relaxed intimate atmosphere. The long horizontal mirrors over the facing bars reflect the lights, slowly rotating ceiling fans, and the customers, to infinity. Two television sets hung high at either end of one bar bring us up short and back to today. A "Born Wicked" banner features Pete's Wicked Ale. The restaurant decor carries the same warm old-time theme with inlaid paneled booths that fit comfortably in their second home. Regular diners find "All You Can Eat Specials" on Tuesday: Chicken Fingers and Wing Dings; on Wednesday, Spaghetti and Meatballs; on Thursday, Fried Shrimp and Clams. The Raw Bar is open Tuesday through Saturday.

The colors maroon and teal prevail in the public rooms and the halls. Upstairs, where guests stay the night or longer, high-ceilinged room 20 has a Lincoln bed and matching dresser. The mattress, I discovered gratefully, is much younger than Lincoln, and firm. On a lace cloth covered table sits a worn red leather-bound *King James Bible*. On another table are issues of *Susquehanna Life* and local journals, along with a copy of a child's *Old Bed Time Story Book*. Outside, through a door under a glass transom with painted floral decoration on the sleeping porch, there's a small white painted iron crib containing a mature, once loved teddy bear. Nothing's fancy. Just what a traveler stopping en route might need to unwind and relax. There's hot water in the bathroom and plenty of maroon and white towels. Outside room 20, on the porch overlooking Chestnut Street, tables with crisp maroon cloths and place settings are waiting for dinner guests. Window boxes overflowing with pink petunias perch on the ledge, hung also with red, white, and blue-swagged bunting. From overhead swings a hand carved brightly painted gilded wooden sign:

Mifflinburg
Hotel - Motel
Scarlet D Tavern
Fine Foods & Spirits

Bill Heim volunteered for Vietnam. He was in the navy and saw three tours of duty. His father had been a prisoner of war in World War II. After the war, Bill tried working in his father's insurance business in Lewisburg, and then tried other things. His family, on both sides, has a long history in Buffalo Valley, the Ruhls and Mitchells and Mensches. He tells an abbreviated ghost story of one of the still existing Mensch family houses, not far away in the valley at White Springs, down the road from the Craft Shop of Jamur's friend, Chester Slokevich. Bill's a Mensch on his mother's side. This was back in the early 1800s. They had a dwarfed retarded boy in the family who was kept in the basement tied to a bullring next to the walk-in fireplace, to keep him out of sight. Legend has it that late at night little Earl's chains still can be heard rattling.

Bill's own large log house, on the other side of Hartleton heading west out of Mifflinburg on 45 just before the Narrows, is on an original William Penn land grant. It was built in 1828, using the corner post technique, and was probably a tollhouse or an inn. At one time Bill raised ducks, chickens, goats, and steer on his acre and a half. Until recently he kept twelve pigs working zealously on the garbage from his restaurant. Their dung fertilized his crops of lettuce, tomatoes, potatoes and carrots; another example of Bill's respect for recycling.

Bill Heim's Log House. Photo by Joan Morse Gordon.

Remnants of Bill's family roots can be found up and down Route 45 in Buffalo Valley, on tombstones and in courthouse records. But Bill had the need to "create a place" of his own. When he opened the tavern in 1978, it was the first bar with entertainment in Mifflinburg. Like anything new, he met resistance from his neighbors. The first year, he was arrested nine times for noise. He brought in jazz and bluegrass bands on the weekends. James Murray, a/k/a Jamur, now a regular customer, came along with a group from Philadelphia known as the 49th Street Band. The lead guitar had to be bailed out of jail to come along and play. He stayed on, too. After a while Bill gave up on the music and put the emphasis on dining, the tavern and the rooms.

Chris Heim started at the Scarlet D as a bartender. She was working the bar when Jamur arrived from Philadelphia, and remembers his blonde girlfriend, Eileen. "He always had his harmonica. Nice, and all that. Different. Kinda weird. At first he seemed like a drunk or druggie. Not lately. Now he only shows up two or three times a month."

Jamur

"James Murray's the name, but you can call me Jamur," he swiveled his bar stool in my direction with an ingratiating smile. "That's how I sign my art work. I do scrimshaw, you know . . . scratching on ivory." I nod as I sip my beer. "It's also called intaglio. But I don't use ivory any more. It's endangered. I use a composite of marble called Kerrico marble they make down in Selinsgrove. Corian works, too." Corian is more usually at home in the Formica world of countertops, although artists have clearly discovered its other virtues. "I did an Iwo Jima in Corian," he continues. "But you have to use a few coats of wax under the ink or else it will soak in and mess up. They used to have these Corian samples . . . ovals." He cradles the imaginary shape lovingly in his hands. "Perfect like ivory for scrimshaw. It's hard to get material now. For a while I used piano keys. I do ships and I do Emmett Kelly, very popular. You know, the clown. I'll get 75 dollars for a Kelly scrimshaw. It takes about four hours to finish one." Where does he sell, I ask, as he pauses to catch his breath? To individual clients, he responds vaguely.

It is early on a Sunday evening in July as I perch next to Murray at the bar of the Scarlet D Tavern, in the Hotel Mifflinburg on Chestnut Street in Mifflinburg (the name Route 45 takes through town). I've made the journey east out of Penns Valley over the Narrows into Buffalo Valley. Murray is a compelling, compact figure with wavy red hair, fair skin and blue eyes, probably in his early forties. His smile is ready, revealing large straight strong teeth. He's wearing an open collared shirt and cut-off jeans. Stationed around us are burly, bare-armed locals sporting baseball caps, drinking beer, and watching a Pirates game on TV.

"I'm Scotch. From Camden, New Jersey. But I've been here since 1980," says he, continuing his monologue. "Camden's where my mother lives, but I don't like it there. When I come back here to Buffalo Valley it feels like mother. Here I'm home. Those sheltering mountains, they remind me of 'nam." Here he pauses momentarily to reflect on a swig of beer. "I'm an artist and at one time I ran out of ideas. But here in the valley I walk outside and look around and I can paint. Georgia O'Keeffe, she taught us a thing. After 'nam, this place is home. Look at Bill, the bartender. He owns this place and a pig farm down the road. He's real. He was there, too. In 'nam. Now I live here in the valley on my farm. I've got ten Appaloosas and a herd of dairy cows."

Jamur's on a roll. I don't interrupt. "I'm better than Picasso," he continues. "He tried ceramics for one year. I did them here for three years. Worked with a woman down the road right here in Mifflinburg. Ran the kilns. Three firings in one day! I didn't use the wheel. Worked with slabs of clay. We made decorated baskets and buttermold tiles. And I had complete freedom to use any colors. We were very successful. Sold to Bloomingdale's, Neiman Marcus." Why did it end, I manage to ask? A divorce. Her husband got the business. "I'm doing a portrait of her now. Impressionist. There's this scene with her sitting in front of a pond. In back is a sky blue-white. She's sitting surrounded by lots of the pots I made."

How did he wind up in the valley, I ask sipping on my Iron City Light? "I had a gig here at the Scarlet D one weekend in 1980. I play the harmonica, you know. The second night a beautiful blonde came in. I stayed. We lived together for eight years." They're no longer together. "Now she's my best friend. And music and art are my wives. They're in my name, Jamur." I don't quite get it but don't want to interrupt the flow.

He rambles on. I'm on my second beer. I don't know how many he's had. "I've been all over. I wish I could get some third world people to do my scrimshaw for me. I'm a fetishist, too." I don't challenge that remark, or others, the way his mind jumps around. "When I was in Albuquerque I worked in turquoise and other stones. My brother-in-law and I, we used to do collage and assemblages like Dali and Duchamp. We found things along the beach. I'd like to live to be 150. I have so many things I want to do." Looking like a full-sized version of a leprechaun he smiles and takes another swig of beer. His enthusiasm is contagious. I relax. He rambles on.

Jamur has been sitting at the Scarlet D bar for quite a while, frequently urging Bill Heim to refill his own pewter tankard. "I better take the back roads home tonight," he mumbles. "I don't want to be stopped for drunken driving. Never been stopped before. Never been arrested." After a swig and a pause, his mind is somewhere else. "It's bad in Cancun." Somehow Jamur is suddenly transported to Mexico. "If they catch a guy drunk they force his head back and pour Coca Cola up his nose. Maybe that's what they think snorting coke means!" He's pleased with his little joke. "Cancun, that's a bad place. I'll never go there. You know, the Mayans, they used human blood to bind their bricks to build their cities. Gutters running with blood. I was planning to go. A friend gave me a ticket. I turned it back to the airlines. I gave it away when I found out about the blood. No, I'll never go there." Jamur's had this kind of horrible feeling before. Once he went to the Metropolitan Museum in New York and was bowled over by a Breughel painting. It was so raw! "The back of my head got hot. I wanted to shout out." He's had visions before. In one he was where his friend Linda Buchanan now lives in Lower Fort in Woodward in the 1770s, and was caught in the Indian massacre. It was a horrible dream.

Jamur's home is a few miles south of Mifflinburg in gently undulating farm country south of Penns Creek in Snyder County. It looks a lot older than its 70 years. The barn has collapsed to one level, with hay coming through the top. The porch is sagging, its roof held up by hollow round columns. "Bluebird condos" he calls them. "When I replace these, I'll drill some new holes for the birds." Inside, the walls are covered with his artwork, paintings and scrimshaws. Pointing to an oil painted on an ironing board cover, Jamur explains that his inspiration was a photo of a calendar girl for a ball bearings company. "I call her Jerseytown girl. She is the spirit behind bluegrass."

He explains that on Wednesday nights "pickers," mandolin and guitar and banjo players, as well as fiddlers, come out of the hills to this bar outside of Danville at the Jerseytown Inn, and really let go. Jamur is the only harmonica player. Sometimes there's a washtub and a bass. "It's a cornfield of guitar necks, Jerseytown farmers, Appalachian in their DNA," he explains. Sometimes four generations together, they even "lay down" Mozart. The bar is incised with woodburned designs and there are paintings on the ceiling. To Jamur, it, too, is like going home.

Near his workbench is a scrimshaw relief of the frigate Constitution. His tools are carbide tipped scribes, but he also uses ice picks and dental tools. Right now he's working on a rhinoceros. First he gouges with his scribe on top of the sketch he's copied from a photograph. Then, using black waterproof ink number 4415, he wipes it on and wipes it off, leaving threads of ink in the grooves.

Jamur has never had formal training but traces his interest in art back to the third grade. That's when he started reading about art. He reads a lot now, too, he tells me, including *Art Business News*, which alerts him to his competition and clues him in on what other artists are up to. He figures there are probably 8,000 artists as good as DaVinci and Michelangelo. In *My Life with Picasso*, Francoise Gilot discusses the engraving technique, he tells me. "You always have to have a focal point in an art piece. In this rhino it's the eye."

Jamur snorts in annoyance. He has forgotten to record the time he started. That's how he knows how much to charge. He's planning to make another rhinoceros as barter for his dentist's wife who collects them. He found a good image in an old book. At his last dental visit Jamur brought a scrimshaw giraffe as a gift in addition to his payment. "My scrimshaws, they're coins, ducats, bargaining chips," Jamur proclaims proudly.

Surrounding him are more scrimshaws of sailing ships, a round Little Red Ridinghood, and an oval Alice in Wonderland amid falling playing cards, which he thinks is based on a drawing by Ruskin (I think it's Tenniel), and a Charlie Chaplin from a Hirschfeld caricature. He describes them as hand-etched art on cultured marble. Does he ever question whether his work is original, I inquire? "Is Warhol original?" he counters.

Jamur's been living in the house for six years. He shares the rent with a roommate he considers morosely, but momentarily, a deadweight. The herd of Ayreshires and Appaloosas, it turns out, are part of the view he enjoys on the steep sloping hillside. The cattle are not his. A neighbor owns them.

Looking reflectively out of the window he says again that the landscape here is like 'nam, where he spent 11 months in the hills. It was hot like summers here in Buffalo Valley, but the vegetation was something else. He was with the 31st Engineers and flew helicopters every day for six months. He hitchhiked all over, most of the time by helicopter and most of the time without a gun. "I always saw the beauty. After the war we thought it would be a new Hawaii." Jamur says he's working on a book covering the time "from 'nam to now." But he's not yet sure if whether he has to bring in the future. "All the names are changed," he advises me, reassuringly. "It's almost culminated."

Jamur has devised a trademark, like Whistler's butterfly, which he incorporates into many of his paintings. It's a flying rose. "Bikers like it for their T-shirts, he says." Most of his images he gets from photographs and frequently uses composites from different photographs. Here's one of contemplating hands that he calls "At the Butchering."

Leaning against the wall is the portrait he's doing of Andrea West, his ceramist friend and former boss. It's taken from an enlarged 1980 slide. A fairly flat two-dimensional figure sits near a flat painted pond surrounded by bright colored clearly defined large ceramic baskets in the shape of pigs, geese and chickens. These baskets and tile, based on old wooden butter molds, were Andrea's best sellers. Jamur has a full set of the butter molds with designs of wheat sheaves and other early American motifs.

"Painting," he muses, "that's pure art." It seemed to him like Pompeii, like a tomb, he remarks, in another non sequitur. Here he points out that he has incorporated Jackie O's eyes into Andrea's face. It was while working for Andrea that he started painting. "When you're trying to survive, art and music isn't a bad way. They are escape windows you give people. You see the smiles and hear the laughter."

After graduating from high school in Merchantville near Camden, New Jersey Jamur tried his hand at pumping gas, worked in a stable and finally sold music in a department store. He then joined the Marine Corps and was trained as a helicopter pilot to serve in Vietnam. "At 18, 'nam was high adventure. Some people never had adventures," he says wistfully.

In 1974, after the war, under the GI Bill, Jamur was accepted at the University of New Mexico and took a course in jewelry making and drawing. "You had to draw a fender and a tire. I guess—for perspective," But he "hit a bump" when he had to take a math course. So he dropped out of school but stayed in the area working in jewelry with turquoise and then ivory. About that time, while excavating for the Alaska pipeline, workmen were digging up the teeth and tusks and bones of mastodons and mammoths and fossilized walrus, as well as hippopotamus and whale teeth. With that wealth of material available Jamur started his scrimshaw in earnest.

After a while he drifted back east to New Jersey and got a job in construction, learning masonry and carpentry. "Utilitarian art work," he calls it. Working conditions were pretty rough, so he headed down to Tennessee where things weren't much better. At one point he "lived on grits in Knoxville for two weeks," he remembers ruefully. He then found his way back into his old love, music. His grandfather had played the harmonica, and Jamur picked up the piano and guitar by osmosis by listening to albums. He got himself a job in record distribution, which eventually led to the 49th Street Band, and finally his arrival in the valley.

To supplement his income from his art, Jamur tends bar at the Bull Run Inn in Lewisburg. He specializes in banquets, wedding rehearsals and class reunions. It's easy money for him at 15 dollars an hour and good tips. "I'm an honest bartender. I ain't a thief. That's why I'm hired," he assures me earnestly. Chris Heim mentions that these occasions are formal. Jamur has to wear a tuxedo. "They call him James and he seems to like it." He thinks that being Catholic was the clincher in getting the job. Back in Merchantville, New Jersey at St. Peter's, Jamur was an altar boy who drank wine in the sacristy. But not now, when he's on duty.

When he can, with his bad back, Jamur still does some carpentry and masonry. He has a service connected disability caused by a 20 gallon drum that hit him when it fell from a helicopter in Vietnam, so he is entitled to free medical care at the Veterans Administration hospital in Lebanon near Hershey, Pa. Last year, he tells me, he went back for a reevaluation. The heated swimming pool and golf course were fine, but the food was atrocious. To see if he was suffering from Post Traumatic Stress Disorder, he stayed there for two weeks of physical examinations and written tests. The additional pension, if he were eligible, would leave him more time for his art. Testing for the effect of Agent Orange with only a few questions, blood pressure and blood tests, Jamur feels the whole procedure was a farce and a smoke screen. "All the boys who actually had it are dead," he observes ruefully.

Jamur's painting style is consistently flat. Texture doesn't concern him. Nor do color values or composition. But he never forgets his focal point. That's a given. As with his scrimshaw, he does what he likes or what someone will pay for. He doesn't mind sharing the credit. Leaning against his studio wall is "Bill's Whitewater Review," a painting of President Clinton playing the saxophone in his shorts. "A lady did the background," he acknowledges, giving credit to an unknown collaborator.

Another leaning painting is the waist-up portrait of a dark-haired smiling man, obviously copied from a photo. "This is Linda Buchanan's father. Neat gal, you'd like her. In fact, why don't you bring it to her if you're heading that way," he suggests. A good excuse for us to meet. He tells me Linda lives in Penns Valley about 15 miles west, in a compound dating back to Revolutionary War time. Jamur's mind jumps around again. He picks up a painting of sunflowers to show me. "I tried to beat Vincent here. Do you think I succeeded?" he asks.

Chester

"In the morning I'm 49, in the evening I'm 99," says Chester Slokevich, with an almost toothless smile. Wispy white hair in disarray, bared to the waist, his pinched shoulders and sagging flesh confirm that he's getting on toward early evening, hovering in the lower 80s. He sits on the steps of his house-cum-shop which crowds in on the White Springs narrow crossroads corner along Reuben Haines' original road taken by Aaron Levy on the way to his new town. We are both watching his friend Jamur attempt to fix the water pump for the well in his front yard. "I was all over two counties hunting for parts for that thing," Chester explains, with a slight indeterminate accent. When he finally found the part he needed, he struggled at it alone, eventually realizing his need for an extra pair of hands to do the job. Just about then, Jamur happened by to show me his friend's woodcarvings. Jamur turns quiet in Chester's presence and goes about his business helping his friend.

Since his two carpal tunnel operations Chester can only work at a strenuous clip for an hour at a time. Even then, detail is hard. From the enlarged knuckles on both hands it is apparent that arthritis adds to his problems. Thick lens glasses don't help either, when you earn your livelihood making fine repairs as a Mr. Fixit.

Jamur and Chester. Photo by Joan Morse Gordon.

Until the winter of 1994 when the roof of his barn collapsed, forcing him to move everything it contained into his small, low-ceilinged 90 year-old house, Chester ran an antiques business in the barn during the day and an antiques repair business in his house at night. He's slowly rebuilding the barn roof by himself and complains about the rising cost of two-by-fours and lead roofing nails.

His faded shingle reads "Chester's Craft Shop, R.D. 1, Mifflinburg." He's still open for business but admits, "I'm a character, a hoarder. I know it's a sickness, but I won't sell, or at least I make it difficult." For reasons only he knows, potential customers are adversaries and he feels they're only out to dupe him.

Every inch of the house—floor, walls and ceiling, including the kitchen and bathroom, distinguished only by their camouflaged appliances, are covered with things. His own creations, and a pack rat collection of everything else imaginable, are cluttered but clean. "Hello my name is Chester," reads a label from a recent bus trip on the refrigerator, near other labels for Amnesty International, Greenpeace and The Nature Conservancy.

Gingerly picking one's way through the rooms, a potential buyer would come across a reproduction of Aaron Burr's desk, made from a blueprint by Chester; an 1890s clothes washer; small wooden Aztec temples (from his imagination); three and one-half foot papier maché half-a-woman lamps, consisting of shapely legs with garters (he made 12 for a barroom in New York which have since been moved to the French Riviera); a brightly painted carousel horse, sheriffs' badges, sleigh bells, a wasp's nest, Buddhas, carved coconut shells, old bottles, a cuckoo clock, a steer's skull, old Coke signs, a toy fire engine, an Atlas-supporting-the-globe clock, a plaster Arc de Triomphe, Mickey Mouse, Betty Boop, Felix the Cat, a Wonderful Wyoming trivet, tiles, thimbles, spoons, King Kong, beer steins, a set of Jamur's friend, Andrea West's butter mold tiles, 90 teapots and 500 assorted collector plates, many still in their original boxes.

"I can fix anything if you pay for it. But if you want it tomorrow, forget about it," Chester announces, almost belligerently. He used to weave baskets but his arthritic hands can no longer maintain the necessary tension. Still, he works in wood in a small area cleared on the first floor, using anything he thinks suitable for a tool, from an 1810 lathe and a jig saw, to a pie crust edger.

Working with wood, he carves his own version of Native American masks, and turns objects like a two-foot long upholstered "fainting couch" on whim. He has a few long-standing orders for the couches. Also in demand are saltboxes, sconces, frames and dolls houses. On the ceiling over his work area hangs a four-by-seven foot framed wooden jigsaw composition painted in clear primary colors. He's particularly pleased with these abstract designs. Smaller versions are hung throughout the house. What "they" want is what he'll make. Once it was a table with a marble top to dance on. "Oh, dose legs," groans Chester, remembering how hard it was to make them strong enough.

He already knows what his next project will be after the barn roof is done. Enthusiastically, he demonstrates to me by cutting a large triangle out of paper and rolling it into a cone. This he will translate into wood, turning it on his lathe, cutting, angling and mitering, making a horn-like sculpture all in the round. Another idea for abstract jigsaw puzzles for children to paint and assemble grips his fancy. "Am I a genius or a dope?" he asks slyly, and seems to know the answer.

Upstairs, in his "cozy corner," is his collection of 3,000 78-rpm records, mainly opera, Puccini and Verdi. He owns two "His Master's Voice" original wind-up phonographs. One, with a richly patinaed inlaid wooden horn, takes one-quarter inch thick records; the other is a 1902 cylindrical Bakelite disc player. He greatly prizes a collection of records by the scarcely remembered soprano, Jessica Dragonette. Chester is in love with her voice. Many years ago, when she had a weekly radio program, he called the station just to talk to her, but never got through. Jeanette MacDonald and Nelson Eddy are other favorites. Chester owns 15 out of 17 videos of their old movies, including "Naughty Marietta." "Two more to go," he promises.

His library runs to science (*Astrophysical Concepts*), murder (Agatha Christie) and mayhem, "The more blood the better!" he says gleefully, rubbing his gnarled hands together. On the ceiling of this bedroom area are a scary collection of knives, sheathed and unsheathed, and a selection of crucifixes. The painting of a nude, by his friend Jamur, hangs on the wall. Under the bed he has stashed 20 dolls. On another shelf are a wide variety of clockworks. He has a standing order at the mint for all new issues to add to his substantial coin collection. What does he collect, I ask him? "Anything bizarre, erotic and neurotic," he admits.

It's easy to imagine the delight his grandchildren take in rummaging through his treasures. One night, after they had visited, Chester says he was awakened by an intermittent low moaning sound he didn't recognize. Across the road is the Mensch mansion, said to be haunted by the same little Earl known by Bill Heim at the Scarlet D in Mifflinburg. Chester's first uneasy thought was that the ghost of the legendary retarded dwarf was haunting him. But the eerie sound was closer at hand. Finally, he found its source—the old disc phonograph player that the children had wound up earlier that day and forgotten to turn off.

Chester's gardens behind the house are steeply terraced with railroad tie steps, and are divided into many nooks and crannies. Undoubtedly, they have seen better days. Small outbuildings, including a privy, are covered with Andrea's brightly colored butter mold tiles. Empty birdcages and iron rings hang from trees. A nine-foot Wizard of Oz tin woodsman flanks a garden corner; his arms are dryer exhaust tubing, his eyes bottle caps. There had been a companion straw man who didn't survive the harsh winters. Chester favors witches, both good and bad. Some of his customers have gotten into the spirit and brought them witchlike clothes. His strawberry angel who floated over the strawberry patch to discourage birds was made of a flimsy cloth. She, too, could use a refurbishing. A black Styrofoam obelisk "sentinel," inspired by Arthur Clarke's *2001*, patiently awaits a signal from Jupiter. It stands near an icebox and a privy he's storing for his friend, Mrs. Musser.

All manner of containers in pottery and metal are planted with surprise treasures. Many years of thought and invention have been lavished here in the multi-level garden, but the winter of '93 froze out a long tunnel of honeysuckle and devastated other carefully nurtured plants, dampening their gardener's enthusiasm and discouraging his limited energies.

Chester's taste runs to the exotic in flora, with a wide variety of herbs, tulip vines, kiwi fruit and Chinese plums probably not seen anywhere else in Buffalo Valley. Friends supply him with cuttings and he regularly receives catalogs of rare seeds and plants from around the world. Paths are controlled with cut-off half tires. An unusual purple "victory" plant, and patches of asparagus, horseradish, rhubarb and blackberry line them. This year, adding to the problem of a premature frost, he didn't get around to spraying. As a result he had no plums or peaches

But he did have black walnuts. The ground is littered with them. Down the road, he points, is a central receiving station for black walnuts. Last year, Chester picked a couple of hundred bags. Not this year. He claims that he didn't even make a dollar an hour. "Pickin' 'em,

Chester and Friend. Photo by Joan Morse Gordon.

takin' 'em up to him, waitin' until he hulled 'em and all that . . . I got two dollars and forty cents!" But this year he will dry some walnuts and use the hulls for a rich black stain. When his wife was alive, he'd line up a few bushels of walnuts in the road and run over them with the truck, and "they'd hollow out real nice." The dryer they were the better they'd hollow. They're really good, he insists. But now, he admits, he has no teeth with which to eat them.

"Do you like a drink now and then?" he asks me as we set for a spell in the crowded kitchen, after climbing around the garden. I nod yes, questioningly. Rummaging under the sink, he emerges with a filled plastic gallon jug, one of 40 he has on hand. Yes, Chester also makes wine, 17 kinds, "garbage wine" he calls it, out of almost anything around. Nettles, for instance, and mint, rhubarb, elderberry, blackberry, apple, cherry and plum. He learned how from a pamphlet. He pours some wheat wine, vintage 1981, into a crystal cordial glass for me to taste. It's really quite good, I tell him. "I don't drink, just nip," he confides. His perforated ulcer, you know.

This wine venture was inspired by his friend, Mrs. Marie Musser, who arrived one day with a load of old green jars which she wanted to keep. Chester was to dump the contents on his compost and return the empties. But first he tasted the old peaches, plums and berries and thought they were still good. So he kept the fruit, but dumped the vegetables. When he was young, his father had made cherry wine and vodka, he remembered, so why shouldn't he try, too.

Winemaking is serious business, Chester tells me. He's very precise, no guesswork. Add the appropriate amount of sugar to your base, stir it every day morning and night, and keep it warm. Then you strain and bottle it, topping each bottle with a bleeder, a plastic or metal gadget that allows the gas to escape. One hitch was that the bleeders cost about four dollars apiece, so Chester figured balloons might do as well. Nickel balloons proved to be the best. Penny ones were too small. For some reason the nickel size weren't available one year when he needed them. But Harold Musser, Mrs. Musser's late husband, saved the day. He brought Chester a bunch of condoms. "They worked perfectly," he says with a Cheshire cat smile, "but I couldn't allow any lady visitors in the room until the wine was ready!"

I am curious to know what brought him to Buffalo Valley. After finishing high school during the depression, he tells me, with no job prospects in sight, Chester came to Poe Valley to work at a Civilian Conservation Corps camp, one of many established under Franklin D. Roosevelt's New Deal program to find work for unemployed city youths. CCC boys planted trees, cleared roads and fire lanes, built parks and lake dams. He liked the Poe Valley camp, which was beautifully located in the heavily wooded setting near Penns Creek, even though he had to live with "Hunkies, Polacks, Dagos and Lithuanians who spoke bad English."

Enlistment was for six months, and later for a year. But Chester liked it so much he stayed on from 1934 to 1938. As part of the training Chester was required to take two courses, typing and first aid. He wound up with two Boy Scout merit badges in first aid. Sixty years later he remembers with pride the 97 he got on a test. More important to his future was the carpentry and turning on a lathe he learned at the CCC camp.

During the monthly dances with girls from the area someone had to be on duty to guard the narcotics at the hospital, and Chester was it. Since he missed the dance, his friend, Watson, arranged a blind date for Chester with Violet Joanna Hosterman, from nearby Woodward. As a girl she had waited tables at the Woodward Inn, owned by her family. On their first double date his Model A Ford broke down in Millheim, much to both men's embarrassment. Eventually, the two couples married.

When Chester first arrived at the CCC camp his pay was $30 a month, of which he and the other boys kept $5 while $25 was sent home to their parents. By the end of his time at the camp, Chester was earning $100 a month. Not a bad income for an unskilled young man in the depths of the depression, and sorely needed by his family.

Chester's father was a Polish army officer who came from a family of soldiers. He came to the United States from Vladivostok in 1911, alone and illiterate. It would be five years before his wife-to-be arrived at Ellis Island, her money sewn securely into her clothes. Chester's version of the immigrant story has "all these here Hunkies and Huns and Russians and Wops" arriving on the same ships used to transport slaves from Africa. I note the irony in his reminiscences, given his own reaction during his CCC year to sharing quarters with "Polacks," among others.

According to Chester, the Statue of Liberty's plea was "to bring all your sick and lame and lazy and you take care of them, brother." And of Ellis Island, "if you wasn't robbed or raped or anything like that, that was the worst place a person could go to, if you was alone." Bitterly, he asserts that it was the ship companies that wanted the fare, wanted to know how much money you had, and shortchanged you in converting zlotys and rubles. "If you got ten cents on the dollar you was lucky. Of course, that's the American way!" Not too different from the plight of the early Palatine immigrants.

When father Slokevich didn't find gold in the streets of New York, as he had been promised, he wound up working the steel mills in Newark. After a while, he left for the coal mines of Shenandoah, where he was actually paid in gold. Chester was born there. When he was ten, they moved to Frackville, PA, where he went to parochial school. That was in 1925. After graduating from high school, and anxious to find work, Chester was told that since they were in the depths of the depression, if you dared to ask for a job, you should be arrested. "With your father working in the mines two or three days a week, you want a job, too?" And so, at 18, Chester went off to the CCC camp in Poe Valley, and found the place where he would spend the rest of his life, except during World War II, when he served in the Philippines for 37 months, ending up as a buck sergeant in the engineering corps. He aided in the capture of 180 Japanese prisoners, he mentions modestly.

Life in Penns Valley during his CCC days had appealed to him and so, in 1943, after his war service was over, Chester came back to Woodward with Violet, working as a pattern maker at an automotive body company that made Bond Bakery trucks. Eventually, he went out on his own briefly with a partner and a patent for a fish pole holder, which somehow grew into a furniture factory in Mifflinburg. Without the safety net of fire insurance, Chester was wiped out when the building was hit by lightning and destroyed in 1965. This was just a year after his wife died, and the year before he lost his son-in law. Chester was destitute and depressed and suffering from perforated ulcers. It took him 13 years to get over the conflux of losses. He is still troubled with occasional bouts of depression.

Enter his "good angel" and friend since 1943, Mrs. Marie Musser, who bought him this house and got him moving again. They first met when he repaired some of her chairs and he has been working for her ever since.

Marie

On a warm summer's day Marie Joanna Montcalm Sexton Purnell Musser greets me at the door of the spacious white clapboard house in Mifflinburg that she shares with her daughter, Joannah. Wearing short shorts and lavender sneakers, Marie Musser walks us briskly through a small room containing an exercise mat and Nordic Track, and seats me comfortably in her compact cheerful kitchen. Sliding doors lead out to a terrace and sunny garden. A diminutive bouncy chatty woman she tells me she's just redone the exercise room and uses it every day. Marie Musser is 91. Shakespeare today would surely agree that age has not withered her infinite variety.

Yes, she tells me, Chester Slokevich is one of her dearest friends. "I'm the only one who fights with him. When he gets enough of me he tells me." She is a loyal friend to Chester, as was her late second husband. And, she assures me, Chester was very loyal to his two daughters and to his late wife, who became drug dependent due to a condition called *tic douloureux* from which she never recovered.

Living alone, Chester protects himself and seldom asks for help, Marie tells me. Just the other evening she brought supper over to him unannounced. In winter he heats his little room and reads and listens to old records. "He knows the classics and lives in a world of culture," she informs me with a sober nod. Sometimes he visits her and pours out everything he's stored up when alone. "Mrs. Musser," he says, "what would I do if I didn't have you to talk to. I feel my time's not wasted."

Marie remembers a while back when, in response to a friend's call, she was summoned to Chester's bedside. She called the doctor who said the patient urgently required seven or eight pints of blood due to his bleeding ulcer. Marie donated seven pints.

The conversation turns to Chester's Craft Shop in nearby White Springs, "Long ago he should have sold and sold and sold. But he's a hoarder!" She sounds exasperated. "He has some great stuff among the trash." Marie should know quality, having run The Little House Antiques for over 15 years. A small separate building next door, it is closed at present, but Mrs. Musser has plans to turn it into a country chair museum. If she says it, you can be sure she'll do it. For years Chester helped repair whatever needed repair including her collection of painted country chairs. Three years ago, at the age of 88, she published her first book, *Country Chairs of Central Pennsylvania*. Many of the chairs in it come from Soper Hollow in Somerset County. They were the creation of early German settlers who lived in isolation, didn't mingle and expressed themselves creatively in their decorated chests and chairs. Art has lived on in painted furniture and Marie Musser has the proof.

Coda

Time passes, and one day I decide to stop in on Chester. Arriving at White Springs crossroads, I am confounded to see his house utterly changed. Instead of the weatherworn boards, the house is sheathed with a totally new skin of shingles. A contractor's truck sits in the drive.

I walk up to the door and peer in. Empty, no trace of Chester or his possessions. The workman hasn't a clue. There's a new owner. Period. Sadly, I realize that Chester is gone, probably dead. Later I drive over to Marie Musser who confirms my fears. Now, I walk up the steep path to his garden. Its outlines are almost obliterated by bramble. On the shed are a few of Andrea West's buttermold tiles. I spy some seedpods, which I pick and pocket, say a silent farewell, and depart.

A litany to the great God Chester
Chester lives with things as songs!
They line his house; they breathe his air.
Chester carves naked women in wood!
They live and breathe.
Chester has a skeleton in his shop,
"His woman," he says.
Chester makes wine,
Green tomato, nettle, grape and plum.
Chester shows me his garden. He grows herbs.
His arbor is lit. He listens to Phillies' games there.
Chester reads astronomy books
He knows the sky.
Chester listens to opera in a day-glo attic.
He invites me there.
Chester serves his communion wine in silver thimbles.
Chester is eighty-three.
Chester carves merry-go-round horses.
He owns one hundred plates.
Chester worked for the CCC.
They brought his wife to him in a cab-over truck.
Chester's house breathes life.
He loves books.
Chester owned a Kandinsky.
He sold it with love.
Chester gives what he is.
Chester lives . . . !

Linda Buchanan
Du Brous Pen Award
Copied, April 4, 1994

Chapter 11

LINDA BUCHANAN AND
LOWER FORT

Linda Buchanan is at home at the farm expecting my visit on this clear July day. To reach her I head my car east out of Aaronsburg along Route 45 onto rolling terrain unblemished by signs of commerce or industry. An occasional Amish horse and buggy skirts the shoulder of the two-lane road. I relax into the slow rural rhythm. Says William Least Heat Moon, in *PrairyErth*, "I like to think of landscape not as a fixed place but as a path that is unwinding before my eyes, under my feet." I pass open cultivated fields and a few widely spaced farms clustered with corn cribs, buggy sheds and vast red barns which dwarf the symmetrical German Georgian farmhouses of brick or mountain stone. Black and white Holsteins rest or graze lazily. Amish homes are easy to spot—no electrical wires, and, until recently no paint. And, in the yard, are white-topped buggies and wash lines strung with dark colored clothes.

At Kraemer Gap, I stop at a narrow dirt lane leading to a farm stand, lured by the sign of "Fresh Produce," offering Indian corn, apples, peaches, tomatoes, zucchini and cucumbers. This is the farm of Stephen Esh, a Lancaster Amish, who settled here in Penns Valley in 1991. Along the lane, I was surprised to see a new white Amish schoolhouse and some fields covered with Agrofabric, a state-of-the-art product used to protect delicate crops. At the stand itself, 13-year-old John Jesse sits behind the counter working with a calculator. I find out he is the oldest of eight Esh children. Flitting in and out of the house and around the barn among the chickens, are smaller Esh boys, suspendered and straw-hatted, and white-capped Esh girls in black dresses, with aprons in purple, lavender, aqua, royal blue and tan. All of them go barefoot. John Jesse tells me that the Eshes also sell mums, pumpkins, gourds, peppers, eggplant, squash and watermelon in season. On the more exotic side, farmer Esh sells miniature goats and white peacocks. I make my purchase of some luscious looking peaches and continue on toward Woodward.

A mountain named Thick anchors the background with the Stover Cemetery at Wolf's Chapel at the road's edge on the right. On this site on December 15, 1789 Jacob Stover "for and in consideration of promoting literature and learning" donated a seven-acre tract "for the use of a school and a master thereof," and a burying ground nearby. Mr. Samsel, the first teacher, taught in German, the predominant language of the settlers. All that remains of the original Stover grant today is the cemetery. Since I'm early for my appointment I stop for a few moments to wander through the old burial ground and try to trace chronologically the settlers' gradual adaptation into an American, English speaking society. I see the alteration of old German family names from Bauer to Bower and Stober to Stover traced from early red shale tombstones with fancy German calligraphy to newer more substantial marble ones simply carved in English. Today the cemetery is conscientiously tended by Edith Stover Smith who lives nearby, and who can trace her ancestry directly back eight generations to Jacob. A marker at the site reads:

ERECTED 1921
1¼ miles S. E. of this spot
stood the lower fort, used
for defense against the Indians
in Penns Valley. Several
persons killed defending the fort
are buried in this cemetery.

*By Bellefonte Chapter D.A.R. and
Col. H. W. Shoemaker*

Linda Buchanan. Photo by Michelle Klein, Centre Daily Times.

Continuing east, on the left, Penns Valley is shielded by modest Shriner Mountain. Ahead looms bold Round Top dominated by the Woodward beacon light. They all merge ahead at Woodward, the eastern end of the valley where the Narrows leading to Buffalo Valley begin. Speckled orange day lilies, fragrant dame's rocket in mixtures of white, pink and lavender, regal Queen Anne's lace, creeping lavender colored crown vetch and nestling purple clover fringe the roadside. Not far beyond the cemetery, I make a right turn off Route 45 and head down Quarry Road. The paved road rises and falls and curls on a gentle roller coaster ride over swollen hills that hide, and then suddenly reveal, densely forested mountain vistas. Around the bend another stark white-painted wooden Amish schoolhouse sits alone, save for the boys' and girls' outhouses. Two twists more and I turn right again. Linda's closest neighbors on the narrow dirt road that ends at her property are Menno and Nancy Yoder, a Nebraska Amish family who live in a small pre-fabricated house.

The Buchanan 320 acre complex of log houses and outbuildings is the very same farm described on the Lower Fort historic marker. It is one of the first settlements in the area and predates the Revolutionary War. Adam Stover, brother of Jacob, the first settler in Penns Valley, laid claim to this tract of land in 1775. During the Revolutionary War, Adam was enrolled in Capt. Charles Myer's Company of Rangers on the Frontier for Northumberland County. According to historian Charles F. Snyder, "These were the men who met the Indian on his own ground, often outsmarted him, and saved the settlements from many incursions. The Ranger is indeed one of the greatest unheralded heroes of the Revolution."

Linda's one-room cabin was originally the butcher shop in the Stover settlement. She's added a few aesthetic touches; a picture window on one side, some stained glass up high on another, and a large stone fireplace. Her two mongrel dogs yip a greeting long before she appears at the door. Linda is a small woman, with a healthy weathered complexion, a strong turned-up nose and sun-lightened brown hair hanging straight to her shoulders. Her dark intelligent eyes and smiling face welcome me inside. I am bringing the portrait of her father painted from a photograph by her friend Jamur, and she is delighted with the painting's likeness.

The cabin shelves are overflowing with books and records, essentials to Linda's well-being. On the wall is a Guardian Bodhisattva with a tranquil expression painted by Jamur, her own powerful portrait of her late husband, Norm, and a sign that reads, "Do your socks match?" Running water and electricity, a refrigerator, a radio and record player are necessary to Linda, but not indoor plumbing. Instead she manages with an outhouse and a tin tub. The cabin is quite close to a stream and Linda has been loath to pollute it with sewage. Her sons-in-law, Scot the potter, Tucker the farmer and musician, and Dave the mason, have volunteered to move the cabin far enough away from the stream to add indoor plumbing safely. But so far she has resisted. Her daughter, Molly, has up-to-date indoor facilities just 50 paces up the hill, there to be used in a pinch.

Since we met five years ago, the modern comforts of a telephone, a large wooden deck and a TV dish have found their way into Linda's essentials. The TV dish, she claims to have gotten on a whim, and at times she'd like to yank it out. It can be addictive, suck you right in, she feels. At last report the TV is unplugged. She still values her silence and her space.

Linda and her late husband, Norman, bought the 320 acres of Lower Fort from Johnny Long in 1972. That was the year Richard Nixon was re-elected, a year Linda recollects with sagging shoulders and a discouraged sigh. After considering buying a farm in Nova Scotia to distance them from the then current hostile political climate, they decided there was a strong enough pull to keep them in Penns Valley.

The Beginnings of Lower Fort

Johnny Long's family had been farmers for three generations. His father, Hasten Long, a direct descendant of the first Stovers, was a farmer before him. But Johnny wasn't a farmer, "no agribusiness bug," as Linda puts it. Instead he hunted and fished and spun yarns like the one about the ghosts of a trenchful of Indians who were supposed to have been killed and buried on the spot where one of the farm buildings was subsequently erected. Johnny claimed that because of its lurid location the building was haunted. And so it had been dismantled and rebuilt on untainted ground nearby, in order to escape direct contact with vengeful Indian ghosts. Another ghost, a man in a long frock coat and tall hat, is said by the Buchanans to materialize occasionally, lurking about the farm, but he seems harmless enough. He just lurks.

Johnny Long never traveled outside Penns Valley. He just wandered his 320 acres and kept living on the property until he died, helping the Buchanans after they bought it. After his death, Johnny's wife Marian donated his little green toolbox to the Aaronsburg Museum. Its contents now fill a few glass cabinets which house the earliest known artifacts from anywhere in the valley. Johnny had jumbled together a collection of arrowheads, spearpoints, pottery, beads, a pestle, and shell scrapers without regard as to where he found them. It was an archaeologist's nightmare and a frustration to curator Bruce Teeple.

Adam Stover's farm became known as Lower Fort after the onset of Indian raids prior to The Great Runaway in 1778. It's not a fort in the way we normally conceive of today, but a farm stockaded to protect its inhabitants from threatening marauders. It was said to have been made of 2 ½ foot diameter oak logs, which were less penetrable by bullets than pine, and were slower to ignite. The overall dimensions were 24 feet long by 20 feet wide and 7 to 9 feet high. Major General James Potter, who fought along with George Washington, and was the "discoverer" of Penns Valley in 1759, was overseer of this land as well as his own large landholding, located about 16 miles to the northwest along Route 45 at Upper Fort. These and Fort Watson were the only three fortified farms in all of what, after 1800, became known as Centre County. There is a rock near her cabin that Linda painted red, white and blue on top of which is a sign reading "Sight *(sic)* of Lower Fort, 1776."

It is known that the earliest inhabitants of central Pennsylvania were called Paleo-Indians, gatherers and hunters who followed migratory mammoth, mastodon and bison 11,000 years ago. Temporary prehistoric campsites have been discovered in the general vicinity, but this was not an area for permanent settlement until recent times. Remains of an Indian ceremonial ring can be found off Route 45 west of Penn Hall, near the Sarnows' new restaurant. One can trace the history of early settlement both by the Native Americans, and later by European settlers, by proximity to ocean, lakes, and rivers: areas close to and following water. Water was essential for transportation of people and goods, and as a source of power for mills. The Susquehanna River was at least 25 miles away, so that the local streams and creeks, which were unreliable during a drought, were the sole source of water, fishing and seasonal transportation. Beautiful and fertile and centrally located as Penns Valley was, it was settled only sparsely and later than Pittsburgh, which was much farther west but strategically situated at the junction of three major rivers.

Coming Together

In 1980, after Norman's death of a brain tumor at the age of 46, most of the Buchanan family came together and settled in at Lower Fort with the same communal spirit of the early settlers and the Scottish clan which was Norman's heritage. Not long ago, three generations of Buchanans traveled to Scotland to their ancestral Loch Lomond for the first time. They brought back soil from its banks to mingle with the rich loam of Penns Valley. Although Linda comments wistfully that many of the men strongly resembled her Norm, with his ruddy complexion and red beard, she failed to bring back even one of them as a souvenir.

Today, three of Linda's five children live on the farm. Along with the grandchildren who aren't away at college, that makes eleven family members in all. Three of her four daughters are nurses. Molly, the eldest, lives with her second husband, Dave Atkins, who is a mason and town supervisor, and her two children by Lance Mellon, in the two-story 18th century main house up the hill closest to Linda's cabin.

Molly and Dave are slowly removing the main house's siding to reveal the original log construction beneath. Instead of the usual notched corner logs found in other parts of Pennsylvania, this house has corner posts with mortise and tenon joints, a technique found in some of the earliest Penns and Buffalo Valley

Molly and Dave Atkins' log house undergoing reconstruction. Photo by Joan Morse Gordon.

homes. The logs are held to the post with square locustwood treenails pins, once called trunnels. Locust was tough and unlikely to rot, according to architect Lawrence Wolfe of Millheim. He thinks this system may be unique to the central Pennsylvanian region and was brought here from the German states. Jill and Scot's house is an old dogtrot further up the lane, and Joy and Tucker's is a newer model. Linda's daughter LeeAnn lives in State College, and her son Andrew lives in Hershey, PA.

For three seasons out of the year, most of the family cooperatively farms on 72 acres, with Tucker Paterson, Joy's husband, in charge. He's been farming here for 18 years. For a while, in winter, Tucker concentrated on his band and kept busy with local gigs. Now he drives a Haines County RFD mail route covering four towns, somehow a more reliable form of income. In season, he grows alfalfa, field corn, sweet corn, market vegetables and tons of flowers that they sell at the area farmers markets until Thanksgiving. Standards at the farmers markets are extremely high, permitting only local homegrown produce. At State College, a sophisticated oasis in the area, this includes oriental vegetables, exotic herbs and vinegars, and fresh trout.

On Fridays, the Buchanans truck their produce to State College, and on Saturdays to Potters Mills. Linda does whatever they tell her and helps with any chore when asked. She and the grandchildren pitch in routinely with the picking and selling. This means long hours in the sun. In return, Grandma Linda is paid one dollar a week, and dinners. "They're all good cooks," she assures me, with a wink. This is a family tradition. Norman's father worked for Norman for a dollar a day, and helped them build their stone house in Dubois, PA. Scot Paterson, Jill's husband, has opened a pottery on Plum Street in Aaronsburg, down the street from Bruce Teeple's Aaronsburg Museum, Billy Stover's log cabin, and across the way from the Randall Stovers. Linda and the grandchildren help out at the pottery, too.

On her walks around the farm, Linda has picked up interesting pieces of hardwood from which she carves walking sticks, embellishing them with shards and crystals she finds here and there. "They seem to lend a certain power," she tells me, referring to her trust in the mystical crystals. In her spare time Linda writes poetry and serves on the boards of the Aaronsburg Library and Museum.

Until recently Linda had a cow, Holly, a four-year-old Jersey, who stayed in the old barn, which was built, it was said, with rounded corners so there'd be nowhere for the devil to hide. Out in the pasture, she showed me that Holly lacked a right rear hoof. This handicap would certainly have led to her abuse or death by the herd, but had no bearing on Holly's milk productivity. Linda found her good company. It was a kind of "discipline and soothing," she says, the rhythm of grooming and feeding grain and hay and water in the morning, and hay and water at night. In return, Holly produced six quarts of milk a day, which Linda turned into yogurt and skir, an Icelandic beverage. Holly's productive life ended abruptly when, during a sudden sky-blackening storm, a bolt of lightning struck a wire fence against which Holly was standing. Soon Linda plans to buy two young heifers and start over again.

Linda has worked with cows since she was 17. Even though she was a city girl from the small community of Dubois, she always wanted to be a farmer. Norm grew up on a dairy farm. She learned from him, helping out on summer vacations. "Him I loved, and the farm I loved as well," she confides. According to Linda, Norman had a basic goodness that never varied. Others I've spoken to, not related to Norm, say the same thing, praising his consistent generosity. The couple met when she was 15. They married when she was 17 and he was 19. That summer they built a little stone house on his parent's farm about seven miles north of Dubois, in a Scotch-Irish farming community.

Despite the odds, Linda and Norman's marriage worked well. As an only child, her parents weren't too happy at her choice of a husband. They could only envision a hard life ahead. They were right, but it was what Linda wanted and never regretted. The Buchanans were a family of seven by the time Linda was 22. "It was a good thing," she says of her marriage. "The kids kinda knew that, too."

It took Norm three years to get his bachelor's degree, followed by a master's in engineering. He taught engineering as a career, but his first love was still farming. When he started teaching at Penn State, Norm and Linda moved from Dubois to State College. Linda says she did "all the suburban things you're supposed to do," like Girl Scouts and PTA, although both of them were longing to get back to farming. Norman was a good father, but firm. He insisted that the children work and do useful service. All of them finished high school a year early and worked for the following year to get their feet wet in the world, before going off to college. Finally, the Buchanans had enough money saved to buy a farm in Penns Valley, in the area near Coburn, originally called the Forks, since it was the point of convergence of Penns, Elk and Pine Creeks. Norm and Linda started out buying calves and raised them to milk cows. The kids helped a lot.

After a while, they bought another farm nearby, keeping the first one for hay and heifers. Its homestead was a handsome Georgian-style brick farmhouse now owned by an Amish family, the Sam Zooks. At one time it belonged to Meyer Hosterman, whose family's name rivals that of the Stovers for longevity in the valley. The Buchanans bought it from an Amish family, the Menno Zooks, who were moving down to Snyder County, at a time when Amish families were in flux and moving frequently. The sale was an unusual event, since Amish sell to their own kind, not to "Englishers," the term they use for anyone who isn't Amish. Nowadays, the Amish are the principal buyers of farms from the "Englishers." With large families and a tradition of giving farming land to their children when they come of age, the Amish have become a prominent presence in Penns Valley.

When Norm and Linda first saw the brick house, it was empty. It was bare, beautiful and stark. That's what it's like again today. The previous Amish owners thought it most important to show the Buchanans the basement first for its large summer kitchen with a spring flowing through it. This source of water would have been of prime importance to settler farmers when they were under siege from Indian attacks. The Zooks thought the Buchanans would be interested in the taste of the cold spring water, as if that alone would sell the place. And it did, partially, Linda admits.

The house had no electricity, so the Buchanans lived in it for nine months with only the use of a hand pump. Norm and Linda started out with forty heifers and two fresh cows. As their first improvement, they electrified the barn because of the cows, whose comfort took priority over the family's. Next came an indoor bathroom (the ubiquitous Randall Stover tended to that). The house never had central heating, so they depended on wood stoves to keep warm. And that's where they raised their family. Eventually they bought Linda's present farm at Lower Fort. When you have dairy cows you have a lot of young cattle and need extensive pasture, Linda explains, so you keep on buying more land.

The Brick House

In
  The great
  Brick
  House
    Kitchen

The
  Walls white
  Smoke
  Toward
    Cream,
And
The
    Multiple
    Spirits
    Smile
    And
      Laugh,
As
The
  Wood
  Fire
    Crackles
    Toward
    Love.

Linda Buchanan 1991

The Sam Zooks

Today, its current owners, a Nebraska Amish family, Sam and Barbara Zook, and their six children, four girls and two boys occupy the brick house. One day Linda takes me by for a visit. I see it has returned to its former state. The electricity added by the Buchanans has been removed, as is the Amish custom. Inside, the wide pine floorboards reflect light in their high polish. The few fine pieces of wooden furniture are handsome, functional and homemade. There are chairs for sitting, but no couches for lounging. The effect is bare and beautiful and stark once again. And serene, the same inner stillness one finds in Shaker homes. I find I am loath to presume by asking questions, and so I remain mute, hiding my pad and pencil. Linda keeps up a cheerful conver-

The one-shouldered suspender denotes a division within the Amish. Note that the ridge-valley geography is evident in the background. Photo by Joan Morse Gordon

sation, while I simply observe. The farmhouse walls are white, the interior door frames pale blue. Barbara and her daughters make quilts or finish quilting tops stitched by others, in a room set aside specifically for quilting. Work is doled out by the piece to many Amish women in the valley by a shop on the main street in Mifflinburg, over the Narrows in Buffalo Valley to the east, which sells the Amish quilt mystique at steep prices.

Barbara Zook, the amply endowed mother flushed with high coloring, and her shy, quiet girls wear identical clothing; purple cotton dresses and royal blue aprons, closed with straight pins only. Starched. Not a wrinkle in sight. Crisp, thin, white muslin prayer bonnets are perched on their smoothly braided long blonde hair. Fine braiding starts at the browline, forming a bun at the nape of the neck. The boys wear black pants and white shirts like their father's. Pale straw boaters sit precariously on their Buster Brown cropped blonde heads. All are barefoot. Sam Zook's flat brimmed hat is black as is his square beard. His upper lip is clean-shaven. It is claimed that Amish men never sport mustaches, since that was the identifying mark of Hessian soldiers in the old country. The Amish have always been pacifists and avoid any hint of militarism. Sam sells the milk from his twelve cows. He tells us he would like some day to have twenty. With the help of his sons, he raises alfalfa, clover, wheat and corn, enough for the family. We thank them for letting us visit, make our farewells and watch as the eight of them wave good-bye from their porch.

Bower Hollow Road, on which the Zooks live, is occupied almost entirely by Nebraska Amish. On Sundays, one sees as many as 30 fragile looking white-topped buggies pulled up in one or another of the neighbors' dusty farmyards, where they take turns holding church services. Although new Amish schools pop up like weeds within walking distance for local farm children, the Nebraska Amish do not build churches. When a community gets too large they clone off into new districts. They build their own schools, adhering to state fire and health codes. As with their homes the Amish schools have no electricity. They take full advantage of available natural light by the judicious placement of the school and the use of large multi-paned windows. And, like Linda, they seem to prefer outhouses.

Linda has a concern for pure water that extends beyond her own land, inspiring her opposition to the limestone quarry in nearby Aaronsburg. Water in the valley now is considered exceptionally clean. She fears that the mining will affect water in the whole area, which is bound to be degraded by the contamination of the aquifers and wells and streams. And oh, the horror of the dust and the trucks and the noise! The family has painted a large sign on the corncrib, in support of the Penns Valley Conservation Association, protesting the quarry:

> "Quarries are the Pits
> Don't Mine Us!"

Come September, the trees take on a rusty, muted tone. The air is still, humid, hazy, intensified by the searing acrid smell of cattle urine and manure. Fields are spent, inhospitable, threatening with sharp, cropped stubble fringed by lavender flax, soft white Queen Anne's lace, rustling goldenrod. Corn stalks dry to a warm gold, the ears a pale papery accent.

Billy Stover

One October evening, the Buchanans pool their resources and invite neighbors and friends to Molly and Dave Atkins' kitchen, to address and collate the Penns Valley Conservation Association's newsletter. Sitting around the kitchen table, young and old help, squeezed elbow to elbow, warmed by the wood stove fire on this cold autumn evening. Molly serves freshly baked zucchini bread and cider as the mailing gets folded and stamped amid the warm and happy chatter. I drink and nibble and add my efforts to the pile.

Joining in the camaraderie of the folding and stamping activities around Molly and Dave Atkins' table in their 1790's farmhouse in Lower Fort is Billy Stover, Randall's distant cousin and near neighbor. Like Randall, Billy is one of the few Aaronsburg old-timers who have been actively protesting the limestone quarry, which he, too, feels, is threatening to ruin the quality of life around Aaronsburg. His view of his hometown is broader than most, looking back with respect to the past, and worrying about the future. Billy's movements are jerky, his neck long and thin and scrawny, like a turkey's. He is all talk and jokes behind his trim white beard and thick glasses. Dot, his second wife, is a perfect complement, round and solid and positive, a clucking nesting hen. Sitting next to him at the crowded table, she tries to protect him against any predatory females and, at the same time, get a word in edgewise.

Billy's family owned the Square Deal garage in Aaronsburg. His father, Vic, was a talented mechanic who fixed farm equipment as well as cars. Vic is said to have been a stern taskmaster who rode herd on his two sons, and was known to have carried a gun at all times. Billy talks on, freely associating, while folding the PVCA newsletter containing the latest ammunition opposing the Confer limestone mine.

When he was small, Billy regales us collators, in order to keep warm at night his mother would give the family heated beans, or a sadiron wrapped in cloth, to tuck under the covers at their feet. The Stover family lived in the kitchen, the only heated room in the house. The "fancy" room with the wood stove was used only on rare special occasions. Billy remembers that when they lived in Coburn, his Daddy, in all seasons, would go out before dinner, cross the bridge at 4:30, shoot a deer and skin it. They'd have it for dinner that very night, by gosh! The game warden knew just what was going on but chose to look the other way. At other times Daddy would return home with a full bag of fish. The family frequently ate flashers, thin slices of potato laid on top of

Dot and Billy Stover. Photos by Joan Morse Gordon.

the stove to brown. From Billy's pleasurable expression in the telling, flashers are a delicious memory. The Stover family outhouse was a two-seater. Billy claims two boys were occupying it when someone shot at random, killing one. "You mean, there was drive-by shooting from buggies in those days?" someone at the end of the table pipes up.

His great-grandfather, Bernard Eisenhuth, lived to be 111, Billy informs us. It is said he voted for both George Washington and Abraham Lincoln. This draws respectful murmurs from the group. "And he didn't run around with wild women," Billy adds with a twinkle directed at a frowning Dot. The Stover (or Stuver or Stober) family came from southern Germany or Austria. Billy's not sure which. It sounds like the Palatine to me. But he is sure it must have been a place that was a lot like Penns Valley. That's why so many of them settled here and stayed.

A handy man like his distant cousin Randall, Billy restored an old log cabin, and moved it to Plum Street in Aaronsburg next to his home. It's not far from the pottery and the museum and library, and just down the street from Randall and Gladys. Billy has authenticated it with his own historic marker reading, "Built in 1811, moved to Aaronsburg in 1987." The cabin came from Millheim, a town one mile to the west, and had belonged to a member of the Musser family, another familiar old German name in the area. It is made of chestnut, pine and oak. Bailer or binder twine, mixed with cement, was used for clinching little blocks between each notched corner log. The roof has split cedar shingles from Canada, and original old glass windows.

You sense the pride in Billy's meticulous recital of each detail. He actually knew the woman, a Mrs. Keene, who was born in the cabin. At one time it was used as a coffin shop. Naturally, Billy and Dot don't live there, it having only one room and, being true to the period, no modern improvements. But they have filled it with authentic 1800s furniture and accessories, and take great pride in showing it off. As I head out in the clear chill night to drive back to town, I can't help but muse on how much similarity in the paucity of creature comforts this settler house shared with the early 20th century house in which Billy spent his youth; and his neighbors, the Amish, share today.

The Fall Festival

Every year, during the Haines County Dutch Fall Festival in October, Billy and Dot open the cabin to the public for free tours, and dress up in not-quite period costumes. This one year, Billy sports a soft-brimmed brown leather hat, jeans, and a loose white top

over a plaid shirt, and beads. White-haired Dot amply fills a long floral-printed cotton gown, and wears a frilled white cap, tied under her chin. Pale blue lace gloves, a loose turquoise cro-cheted shawl, and sensible flat leather sandals, complete her outfit. Dot stands at the cabin door wel-

Evelyn Vonada baking sticky buns for the Fall Festival. Photo by Michelle Klein, Centre Daily Times.

coming visitors inside. Billy has a running spiel to hustle passing tourists inside, and to watch the cider making demonstration outside on the lawn.

The Dutch Fall Festival brings out most of Aaronsburg's 680 residents, as well as hordes of visitors. The word Dutch in the title is a corruption of the German Deutsch, as in Pennsylvania Dutch, relating to the majority of early local inhabitants. Monies raised at the festival go to support the Aaronsburg Museum and Library and Civic Club.

For the two days of the festival, the museum and library are open all day Saturday and Sunday. Upstairs in the library the sun streams through the large stained glass dedicated to Hostermans, Rupps, Krapes and Crouses, families whose history in the valley long precedes the old building.

Locally stitched patchwork quilts, both old and new, are displayed hanging like banners from the rafters. Iva Hosterman, Sarah Fiedler and Marian Bower produce intricate patterns of starbursts and birds, both peaceful and clawed, in red, green and gold; all-white daisies are outlined and signed in blue; one quilt, circa 1900, using odd-shaped patches, is obviously stitched from a family's worn old clothes. Downstairs in the museum, crowded in the low-ceilinged windowless basement, Bruce Teeple enthusiastically explains the workings of some turn-of-the-century tools to an engrossed young family.

If you stick to the activities up here at the museum on Plum Street, and in Wert Memorial Park, further west down Plum Street from the pottery and Billy's cabin, you'll get a strong sense of old valley tradition. South, down the block on Aaron's Square (Route 45), along the entire length of town, the sidewalks are packed with people perusing tightly strung stalls and tables of flea market goods, mainly from out-of-town vendors. A few non-commercial stalls, from groups like the neighboring Millheim Volunteer Fire Department selling raffle tickets, bring us closer to the feel of a hometown.

"Park" is a euphemism, when applied to the Don Wert Memorial; it's more an open field edged with a few small buildings, and fringed with trees. The land was donated to the town by D. Sparr Wert in memory of his son, 1st Lieutenant Donald S. Wert, an Air Force pilot and the only Aaronsburg soldier killed in World War II. His sister, Madalene Wert Vonada Haslop, remembers her brother buzzing Aaronsburg in his B25 Bomber before heading overseas. A memorial plaque, modestly planted, is installed at the western end. The elder Wert is the man who rediscovered Aaron Levy's long lost pewter communion set during renovation of Salem Lutheran Church, thus reviving the legend which led to the Aaronsburg Story.

During the Fall Festival, a stage and chairs for entertainment and long communal tables and benches are set up in the middle of the park. A blue and white striped tent offers some shade. October sunshine and an astonishing cerulean blue sky, with fluffy white clouds, set the perfect festive mood for the crowd. The Deacons of Dixieland, a local group of strong male voices, are harmonizing "Down by the Riverside," while a blacksmith noisily demonstrates forging fire tools in one corner.

There are no bread baking, pickling or grain flailing demonstrations this year. The principal activity seems to be milling around, visiting, and eating. Vendors hawk Fetzer and Swartz's French fries. There are ham barbecue and kraut dogs for the meat eaters. Roasting peanuts flavor the air. Warm apple dumplings, with or without rich vanilla ice cream, draw a patient line of droolers. Even longer is the line for sticky buns—"1/2 doz.—$2.50, 1 doz.—$5.00. Limit—2 pans per person." Edith Stover, who tends the old Stover cemetery, helped make 500 ham pot pies to sell at the museum and library tent. Linda Buchanan prepared vegetable soup and bread pudding, and Michelle Teeple made relish, as well as crocheted potholders. According to Edith Stover, the bean soup, another annual special, tastes better on Sunday. Why? Because Saturday night they threw in the leftover ham!

One small note mars the perfection of the day. There is no activity in the shed. Where, in other years, volunteers wielding long-handled paddles over old oil drums converted to wood stoves stir vats of steaming apple butter rhythmically, all is still. Tacked to a post is the following hand-written note, "Sorry no apple butter this year. Head man had retina of eye replaced . . . has not adjusted to wearing glasses. Hope to be back next year." I do, too.

Chapter 12

END OF A JOURNEY

Commemoration

October 23, 1997 arrives cold and raw in Aaronsburg, unlike the warm sunshine that greeted the thousands of spectators and participants forty-eight years earlier for the Aaronsburg Story pageant. Huddled inside a blue and white striped tent, today's small audience sits on folding chairs facing a head table against which leans a large rectangular shape covered with a royal blue cloth bearing the emblem of the Pennsylvania Historical and Museum Commission. The occasion is the dedication of a Pennsylvania State Historical marker commemorating the Aaronsburg Story to be installed at the eastern end of town on Route 45.

Bruce Teeple, eschewing his habitual baseball cap and overalls for a neat tie and shirt, welcomes about 100 representatives of the state, various races and religions, the university, old-timers, friends and the press. Recalling the pageant as the local historic highpoint almost half a century ago, Teeple notes, "It was probably the only time a true cross-section of Centre County residents worked together on such a scale for such a noble undertaking. And it is that event to which we pay homage today."

After many speeches, the presidents of the Haines Township Fall Festival and Penns Valley Historical Association unveil the large impressive marker that reads:

> *"Aaron Levy, a Jewish immigrant who founded this village in 1786, donated ground for the Lutheran and Reformed congregations here and presented them with a pewter communion set. In remembrance of his generosity, 30,000 people gathered in Aaronsburg on Oct. 23, 1949, for a daylong celebration of religious and racial understanding. It included a huge outdoor pageant on a natural stage just north of this site."*

Teeple concludes: "The lure of this region is in its resistance to radical change. The place teaches us lessons about returns: a return to the values of land, work and community; a return to living relatives and long-departed ancestors; a return to the traditions of neighborliness and self-reliance; a return to life as it should be."

Guests are invited to a reception at the Community Building, where there is a promise of a viewing of "The Aaronsburg Story" film, narrated by Quentin Reynolds, a slideshow of the event by Doris Mamolen, an exhibit of artifacts from the pageant, starring the pewter communion set, and apple dumplings. After a blessing by Rabbi Brown over the dumplings, left over from 2,282 made for the Fall Festival, tireless volunteers Mary Hosterman and Dora Mae Stover, confide that the secret of their lightness is a tablespoon of vinegar in the dough.

Doris Mamolen, center, shows off Aaronsburg Pageant photos to visitors. Photo by Michelle Klein, Centre Daily Times.

Warm dumplings, old-timers scanning old photos. Memories. Gladys Stover finds herself in the finale scene holding a maypole labeled Tolerance. "We walked in and we walked out. But we had to practice a long time," she remembers. Her husband Randall helped haul equip-

Photo by Joan Morse Gordon.

ment and build the stage sets. Dean Krape stood on a hill with his box camera and took a picture of his Pilgrim brother.

I seek out the communion set, hold it once again, and contemplate its journey. On my journey, through Penns Valley and time, I have met some older people whose outlines are clear and strong. I have met some young couples that chose this environment because it gave them space and time, to breathe deeply, to explore their potential, to spread out and to appreciate each other. There were others for whom the Valley was a safe haven, those of fragile ego who would have been lost in the wider world. What drew them, drew me. With both the older and younger individuals, it is their inner fortitude and self-sufficiency I admire the most and from whom I hope to continue to draw inspiration.

A Note to My Readers

My leisurely journey along Route 45 has taken more than five years. Over the course of these years both landscape and people have changed, as have I, but I have not been tempted to revise my text with each new occurrence. Just as photographs exist in stopped time, so must they.

To note just a few changes—on entering Aaronsburg from Millheim one will note that Musick's Cottages are now Schafer's Cottages, Ardranna and Ralph having retired to Centre Hall. And Burt Stover is thinking about selling his store and spending full time on his engineering. Randall Stover has turned over his water dowsing to a nephew but continues full tilt dowsing cemeteries. Jim Murray, I hear, is dealing Blackjack to big spenders at a Native American casino in Connecticut. And Marie Musser, having just celebrated her 98th birthday, is working on another chair book, this time on modern American chairs.

As for Con-Stone, Inc., they are petitioning to blast below the water line while the Aaronsburg houses that sit on the continuation of their limestone ridge shake whenever there's a blast of dynamite. Randall's shop door rattles.

There's a fundraising drive on to build a new library and museum on the site of the *Aaronsburg Story*. The simple wooden model resembles a forebay barn. With a secure haven Bruce Teeple will at long last be able to house more of the valley's artifacts with Aaron Levy's communion set as the centerpiece of his collection.

One change I could not have foreseen was the untimely death of Linda Buchanan on July 29, 1999. She was a young 64.

> Perhaps
> I
>   am
>   chosen;
> If
> so
>   grant
>   me
> Wisdom
> not
>   written,
> Love
> not
>   numbered,
> And
> Time –
>   stopped
> and Enchanted

There's no doubt that between the time I write these words and you read them many other changes will have occurred. And life on the road goes on.

Photo by Joan Morse Gordon.

Your Journey Down Route 45

In my research I was intrigued to learn that the counties on either end of Route 45 were named after two 18th century women; Huntingdon, to the west, after Selina Hastings, Countess of Huntingdon, a titled philanthropist, and Montour, to the east, after Madame Montour, a French-Indian who acted as interpreter and conciliator between the settlers and Indians. The honor paid to these enterprising women, bookending my road as they did, gave an extra bit of sisterly comfort and symmetry to my journey, although one would be hard pressed to find even one countess or French-Indian interpreter along the road today.

As it happened I wound up spending the majority of my time in the middle of the road, in Centre and Union counties. But here I am connecting the people and places about which I've written, and suggesting other places for you to explore on your own. Everyone's journey will be unique. Whether one's interests lie in history, geography, geology, sociology, farming, fishing, antiquing or just meandering and absorbing, it's all there.

The one hundred miles of Route 45 traverse five counties across central Pennsylvania. Since 1994 its full length has been designated The Purple Heart Highway in part in memory of Marine Lieutenant George H. Ramer, a Lewisburg teacher who was killed in the Korean War and who posthumously received the Congressional Medal of Honor and the Purple Heart for Military Merit. This medal was established by General George Washington to honor soldiers wounded during the Revolutionary War, and awarded again after the hiatus of many years to members of the military either wounded or killed in combat. But why here, I wondered? When first I noticed them, the Purple Heart road markers jolted me out of my pastoral reveries, and I questioned the rationale of connecting a peaceful road in the middle of nowhere with the tragic reminder of war. But obviously it had meaning to people along the way. And it has had the positive effect of mobilizing a group called the Friends of the Purple Heart Highway, a coalition of bed and breakfasters and others interested in the preservation of this rural route. Check out www.virtualcities.com/ons/pa/c/as/pac61a1.htm for a fund of information. Boalsburg, which we will meet as we travel east, is the home of the Pennsylvania Military Museum. Another possible justification for the label. So be it.

Starting from the narrow western end of the road in Huntingdon County, trout fisherman will find the finest limestone streams on the Little Juniata River and Spruce Creek, although clear stocked streams with brown, rainbow and brook trout are scattered all along the road. The waters stay warm enough to fish all year round. Spruce Creek, the first town we encounter, counts catch-and-release trout fishing as its principal industry. With catch-and-release the fish naturally have a long life span and it's not unusual to hook a perforated-lipped eight pounder. For a change, in this sporting activity the predators are ospreys and kingfishers, not men.

Except for the George W. Harvey Experimental Fisheries area controlled by Penn State, the access to the rest of Spruce Creek is through private hands. Check locally with Spruce Creek Outfitters, (1-814-632-3071), Orvis' Six Spring Fly Shop (1-877-897-3311), and Paradise Outfitters (1-800-282-5486) for guides, supplies and access; and in State College, Flyfisher's Paradise (1-814-234-4189 or www.flyfishersparadise.com) for guides, supplies and detailed reports on all the local streams. Little Juniata River, and Spring and Penn's Creeks are more accessible on one's own.

The name of Wayne Harpster is potent in these parts as the host to fishermen Presidents Eisenhower and Carter and as the owner of the expansive Evergreen Farm, whose nine silos cluster like San Giminiano defensive towers along Spruce Creek that we follow along on our right for about ten miles.   As the valley widens we pass Indian Caverns (www.indiancaverns.com), the first of three commercial caves along the way; with claims that it sheltered David Lewis and his gang.   There are 152 documented caves in Huntingdon County alone. For serious cavers check the National Speleological Society (www.caves.org).

Patchwork patterns of agricultural research fields under the aegis of Penn State University frame both sides of the road.   For a few days in mid-August during Ag Progress Days they are open to the public (814-865-2081).

Passing through Pine Grove Mills you could digress along Route 26 to visit State College for, among many other things, delicious ice cream concocted at their Creamery.   Continuing on Route 45 you might miss Boalsburg, a charming village that sometime in the past cleverly managed to divert through traffic from its Main Street, which was the old Route 45.   Duffy's Tavern built in 1819 in the town center called "The Diamond," was a coaching stop back then (814-466-6241 or www.duffystavern.com).   According to Dr. Peirce Lewis, Boalsburg "is a fairly intact and highly typical early 19th C. Pennsylvania market town that was overtaken and surpassed by the muscular 20th C. State College."   Outside of Boalsburg see the Boal Mansion Museum and the Columbus Chapel (actually from Christopher Columbus' family castle) (814-466-6210 or www.vicon.net/~boalmus) and Pennsylvania Military Museum (814-466-6263 or www.psu.edu/dept/aerospace/museum). Boalsburg prides itself on being the birthplace of Memorial Day and if you happen to be there on that day, you're in for an old-fashioned, flag-waving, drum-thumping parade.   Traveling eastward you'll pass an unusual circular red dairy barn on your left.   Built in 1910, it is still in use.

Since 1874 in late August, Centre Hall has been the site of the Centre County Grange Encampment and Fair.   Over 2000 farm families hold a sprawling weeklong reunion and campout with inherited tent sites and RVs.   From February to December at nearby Penn's Cave "America's only all-water cavern" (www.pennscave.com) take an hour-long boat ride and learn their romantic Indian legend.   Ahead in Spring Mills on the right, you'll spot the Sarnow's Hummingbird Room restaurant in an 1840s manor house set amongst enormous old willows.(814-422-9025 or www.hummingbirdroom.com).

Approaching Millheim on the left, in a small shopping center hous-ing Hosterman & Stover's hardware, don't be too surprised to see Sri's restaurant, where our Thai hostess can produce a hamburger or pizza or Pad Thai. In the center of Millheim, where the former Nieman's Department Store still stands empty, you'll encounter the only red light in Penns Valley. One mile ahead is Aaronsburg. Its wide main street is spotted with restored log houses. At Stover's store on the left you can still see the center of Pennsylvania marker next to the Coke machine. If you head up Pine Street or Rachel's Way to Plum Street you won't be far from the Penns Valley Historical Association and Library. Museum hours are Wednesdays 7-9 PM and Saturdays from 1-4 PM, or call 814-349-8276 for an appointment. Down the street you might like to look in on Linda Buchanan's son-in-law Scot Paterson's Aaronsburg Pottery, featuring crafts of area artisans. It's open weekend afternoons. And, if it happens to be a weekend somewhere between late September and mid-October, enjoy the old-time camaraderie and apple dumplings at the Haines Township Dutch Fall Festival.

Leaving Aaronsburg and its historic marker behind, the rolling landscape with widely scattered farm clusters looks just as it must have 200 years ago. The road signs cautioning the presence of fragile-looking Amish buggies leaves us unprepared for the anomaly of Camp Woodward, "the world's largest extreme sports complex," where potential young Olympic medallists from all over the world train in freestyle biking, skateboarding, inline skating and gymnastics. Call for more information or to schedule an appointment (814-349-5633 or www.campwoodward.com). The camp is now operating the historic Woodward Inn in the village. Turn off there to the largest cavern along Route 45, another purported shelter for highwayman David Lewis and Indian braves, the Woodward Cave and campgrounds (814-349-9800)

After a few miles over the Narrows, we leave Centre County for Union County and are now in Buffalo Valley, the western part of the Valleys of the Susquehanna, a flatter and more open terrain. When passing through Hartleton go slow. I have heard it is a speed trap. Mifflinburg, where our friend Jamur worked for Design Tiles, houses an interesting Buggy Museum, an authentic 19th century buggy factory (570-966-1355). Freshly painted early Victorian houses with welcoming porches and flower boxes line heavily treed Chestnut Street, Route 45's name as it passes through town. Here you'll find Mary Koons Amish Quilts, an outlet for the piecework done by Barbara Zook and other Amish housewives in the valleys. Bill Heim's Mifflinburg Hotel and Scarlet D restaurant is further down Chestnut (570-966-3003). Altogether Mifflinburg is a pleasant place to take time out in your travels.

Lewisburg is the home of Bucknell University, where one can follow links to the pre-Civil War underground railway (570-577-2000 or www.bucknell.edu). Packwood House Museum, comprised of a cluster of rare three-story 18th century log buildings, and located right along the Susquehanna River, houses a quirky collection (570-524-0323). When we reach Lewisburg we could diverge south along Route 15 to Northumberland to visit the house Joseph Priestley built in 1798 (570-473-9474). Or, if we were to head north on Route 15 and beyond we would eventually arrive at the site of Azilum (570-265-3376 or www.frenchazilum.org), admittedly a long detour. But detour has been the essence of my journey, taking the time and following a whim.

Crossing the Susquehanna into Montour County we follow the road to its end or beginning ten miles ahead. Just outside of Montandon, we come to an octagonal 1835 brick building known as the Sodom school, all that remains of a small community named after its original landowner, Lot Corson.

The abrupt ending of our road at the junction of Route 642 led me to believe that it had been arbitrarily diverted at some point. Backtracking a mile or so, I found a road off to the left (SR 3004) that wove through the small town of Mooresburg. This was obviously our original route. At the end of that road we come out on Route 642 at the site of a one-room schoolhouse museum, a fitting place to start or stop.

Other sources of information:

Bellefonte Tourism Commission
101 West Linn Street
Bellefonte, PA 16823
1-814-353-1102
www.bellefonte.com

Centre County Convention and Visitors Bureau/Penn State Country
800 East Park Avenue
State College, PA 16803
1-800-358-5466
www.visitpennstate.org

Pennsylvania Visitors' Guide
1-800-VISIT PA
www.experiencepa.com

Susquehanna Valley Visitors Center
RR3, 219 D Hafer Road
Lewisburg, PA 17837
1-800-525-7320
www.svvb.com

Buttermold Tile.   Courtesy of Joannah Skucek, Design Tiles of Mifflinburg.

BIBLIOGRAPHY

Barrick, Mac. ed. *German-American Folklore*. Little Rock: August House, 1987.
———*Lewis the Robber: a Pennsylvania Hero in Life and Legend*. Terre Haute: Midwestern Folklore: Journal of the Hoosier Folklore Society, Fall 1994.
Bell, Herbert C. *History of Northumberland County*. Chicago: Brown, Runk & Co., 1891.
Blythe, Ronald. *Akenfield: Portrait of an English Village*. New York: Random House, 1969.
Brener, David A. *The Jews of Lancaster, Pennsylvania: A Story With Two Beginnings*. Lancaster: Congregation Shaarai Shomayim in association with the Lancaster County Historical Society, 1979.
Bressler, Leo A. "Agriculture among the Germans in Pennsylvania during the Eighteenth Century." *Pennsylvania History*. Harrisburg: April 1955.
Brissot de Warville, J-P. *New Travels in the United States of America*. London: Printed for J. S. Jordan, 1792.
Bronner, Edwin B. "The Failure of the 'Holy Experiment' in Pennsylvania, 1684-1699. *Pennsylvania History*. Harrisburg: April 1954.
Chatwin, Bruce. *The Songlines*. New York: Viking, 1987.
Clark, John Ruskin. *Joseph Priestley: A Comet in the System*. San Diego: John Ruskin Clark, 1990.
Clarke, T. Wood. *Émigrés in the Wilderness*. Port Washington, NY: 1941.
Cooper, Thomas. *Some Information Respecting America*. London: Printed for J. Johnson, 1794.
Curran, Alfred A. *German Immigration to Pennsylvania 1683-1933*. Columbus, Georgia: Brentwood University Press, 1986.
Day, Sherman. *Historical Collections of the State of Pennsylvania containing A*

Copious Selection of the Most Interesting Facts, Traditions, Biographical Sketches, Anecdotes, Etc. Relating to its Histories and Antiquities, Both General and Local, with Topographical Descriptions of Every County and All the Larger Towns in the State. Philadelphia: George W. Gorton, 1843.

Faber, Eli. *A Time For Planting: The First Migration 1654-1820.* Baltimore: Johns Hopkins University Press, 1992.

Fish, Sidney M. *Aaron Levy, Founder of Aaronsburg.* New York: American Jewish Historical Society, 1951.

Fithian, Philip Vickers. *Philip Vickers Fithian: Journal, 1775-1776.* ed. Robert Albion and Leonidas Dodson. Princeton: 1934.

Godcharles, Frederic A. *Daily Stories of Pennsylvania.* Milton, PA: 1924.

Gutkind, Lee. *The People of Penns Woods West.* Pittsburgh: University of Pittsburgh Press, 1984.

Haller, William. *The Early Life of Robert Southey.* New York: Columbia University Press, 1917.

Hogan, Edmund. *The Prospect of Philadelphia.* Philadelphia: 1795.

Hostetler, John A. *Amish Society.* Baltimore and London: The Johns Hopkins University Press, 1980.

————*Amish Roots: A Treasury of History, Wisdom, and Lore.* Baltimore and London: The Johns Hopkins University Press, 1990.

Jackson, John Brinckerhoff. *A Sense of PLACE . . . A Sense of TIME.* New Haven: Yale University Press, 1994.

Kent, Barry C. *Discovering Pennsylvania's Archeological Heritage.* Harrisburg: Pennsylvania Historical and Museum Commission, 1994.

Knittle, Walter Allen. *Early Eighteenth Century Palatine Emigration.* Baltimore: Genealogical Publishing Company, 1965.

La Rochefoucauld-Liancourt, Francois A. F. *Travels through the United States of North America the country of the Iroquois, and Upper Canada, in the years 1795, 1796, and 1797.* London: R. Phillips, 1799.

Least Heat Moon, William. *PrairyErth.* Boston/Toronto: Little Brown and Company, 1991.

Lewis, Arthur H. *The Aaronsburg Story.* New York: The Vanguard Press, 1955.

Lewis, Peirce F. "Small Town in Pennsylvania," *Annals of the Association of American Geographers,* v.62, No. 2, (June 1972), 323-351.

Linn, John Blair. *Annals of Buffalo Valley, Pennsylvania: 1755-1855.* Bowie, Maryland: Heritage Books, Inc. (Facsimile Reprint) 1989.

————*History of Centre and Clinton Counties, PA.* Philadelphia: Louis H.Everts, 1883.

Macneal, Douglas. "Introducing David Lewis." *Centre County Heritage,* vol. 24.

————"Amplification: David Lewis in Centre County in 1813." *Centre County Heritage.* vol. 26, no.1, Spring 1989. State College, PA: Centre County Historical Society.

Mitchell, Edwin Valentine. *It's an Old Pennsylvania Custom.* The Vanguard Press, 1947.

Muller, Edward K., ed. *A Concise Historical Atlas of Pennsylvania*. Philadelphia: Temple University Press, 1989.

Murray, Elsie. *Azilum: French Refugee Village on the Susquehanna, 1793*. Athens, PA: Tioga Point Museum, 1940

Murray, Louise Welles. *The Story of Some French Refugees and their "Azilum" 1793-1800*. Athens, PA: Tioga Point Historical Society, 1903.

Park, Mary Cathryne. *Joseph Priestley and the Problem of Pantisocracy*. Philadelphia: Delaware County Institute of Science, 1947.

Peterson, Edwin Lewis. *Penns Woods West*. Pittsburgh: University of Pittsburgh Press, 1958.

Pound, Arthur. *The Penns of Pennsylvania and England*. New York: The Macmillan Company, 1932.

Priestley, Joseph. *Letters to the Inhabitants of Northumberland and its Neighbors*. 1797.

Rishel, C.D., ed. *The Life and Adventures of David Lewis, the Robber and Counterfeiter*. Newville, Columbia County, PA: C.D. Rishel, 1890.

Rush, Benjamin. *His Travels Through Life together with his Commonplace Book for 1789-1813*. George W. Corner, ed. Princeton: Princeton University Press, 1948

Schantz, Rev. F.J.F., D.D. *The Domestic Life and Character of the Pennsylvania-German Pioneer*. Lancaster, PA: Pennsylvania German Society, 1900.

Schumacher, E. F. *Small is beautiful; economics as if people mattered*. New York: Harper & Row, 1973.

Seitz, Don C., editor. *Tryal of William Penn and William Mead for Causing a Tumult at the Sessions held at the Old Bailey in London the First, Third, Fourth, and Fifth of September 1670*. Done by Themselves. Boston: Marshall Jones, MDCCCXIX.

Sister Eugenia. "Coleridge's Scheme of Pantisocracy and American Travel Accounts." In *PMLA*, 45 (December 1930).

Swartz, Virginia M. *Xanadu on the Susquehanna—Almost: The Pantisocracy of Coleridge and Southey*. LaPlume, PA: Keystone Junior College, 1986.

Tanner, Helen Hornbeck, ed. *The Settling of North America*. USA: Macmillan, 1995.

Trego, Charles B. *A Geography of Pennsylvania*. Philadelphia: Edward C. Biddle, 1843.

Warner, Sam Bass, Jr. *The Private City*. Philadelphia: University of Pennsylvania Press, 1968.

Weigley, Russell F. ed. *Philadelphia: A 300-Year History*. New York: W.W. Norton & Company, 1982.

Wilkinson, Norman B. ed. "Mr. Davy's Diary," *Pennsylvania History*. XX, Harrisburg: April, 1953.

Wolf, Edwin 2nd. and Maxwell Whiteman. *The History of the Jews of Philadelphia from Colonial times to the Age of Jackson*. Philadelphia: The Jewish Publication Society of America, 5717-1957.

Wood, Ralph, ed. *The Pennsylvania Germans.* Princeton: Princeton University Press, 1942.

Writers' Program of the WPA in the State of PA. *Pennsylvania: A Guide to the Keystone State.* New York: Oxford University Press, 1940.

Yoder, Stephen L. *My Beloved Brethren.* Nappanee, Indiana: Evangel Press, 1992.

I N D E X

Hoover Woods — land grant

Nazimy — Limestone mining (Bethlehem Steel)
"Steel" Farms

Penn Creek goes to Susquehanna

Spring Mills — Log toll house 1846 > Helen Fahy
                                        Environmental Engin.

ORDER ADDITIONAL COPIES OF

THE ROAD TAKEN
A Journey In Time Down Pennsylvania Route 45
by JOAN MORSE GORDON
(ISBN 0-9711835-1-1)

from THE LOCAL HISTORY COMPANY
Publishers of History and Heritage
www.TheLocalHistoryCompany.com

ORDER FORM - PLEASE PRINT CLEARLY

NAME _____

COMPANY (if applicable) _____

ADDRESS _____

CITY _____ STATE _____ ZIP _____

PHONE _____ Please include your phone number so we can contact you in case there is a problem with your order.

Please allow 2-4 weeks for delivery. Prices are subject to change without notice. US shipments only (call or write us for information on international orders). Payable by check, money order, or Visa/MC in US funds (no cash orders accepted)

PLEASE SEND _____ copies at $19.95 each .... Subtotal: $_____

Add $5 shipping/packaging for the first copy and $1 each additional copy $_____

Sales Tax: PA residents (outside Allegheny County) add $1.20 per copy
             Allegheny County, PA residents add $1.40 per copy $_____

                                    TOTAL AMOUNT DUE: $_____

PAYMENT BY CHECK/MONEY ORDER:

____   Enclosed is my check/money order made payable to *The Local History Company* for the total amount due above.

PAYMENT BY VISA OR MASTERCARD:

Bill my __ Visa __ MasterCard   Account # _____

Expires _____ Name as it appears on your card _____

(Address above must be the same as on file with your credit card company)

Signature _____

Mail or Fax your order to: The Local History Company
(Fax 412-362-8192)   112 NORTH Woodland Road
                               Pittsburgh, PA 15232
                               Or — call 412-362-2294 with your order.

QUANTITY ORDERS INVITED

This and other books from The Local History Company are available at special quantity discounts for bulk purchases or sales promotions, premiums, fund raising, or educational use by corporations, institutions, and other organizations. Special imprints, messages, and excerpts can also be produced to meet your specific needs.

For details, please write or telephone:

Special Sales, The Local History Company
112 North Woodland Road, Pittsburgh, PA 15232,   412-362-2294.
Please specify how you intend to use the books (promotion, resale, fund raising, etc.)